SITTING STILL
With Twilight Owls

SITTING STILL
With Twilight Owls

exploring the web of life
on San Juan Island

SUSAN VERNON

ARCHIPELAGO PRESS
Friday Harbor, WA

SITTING STILL WITH TWILIGHT OWLS
exploring the web of life on San Juan Island
Copyright © 2023 by Susan Vernon
All Rights Reserved

ARCHIPELAGO PRESS gratefully acknowledges
the support of Robert E. Frey for the publication of this book.

Photos by Susan Vernon
Cover and interior design by Rebecca Cook
Map illustration by Rebecca Cook

ISBN: 978-0-9653185-3-2 (paperback);
978-0-9653185-4-9 (e-book).
Library of Congress Number: 2023914852

Published in the United States of America

First Edition

ARCHIPELAGO PRESS
P.O. Box 3081, Friday Harbor, WA. 98250
arcpress@rockisland.com

*Cover photos: (front) short-eared owl. Left to right: satin flower, western bluebird,
western tailed blue butterfly, red fox. (back) Douglas fir, sand-verbena moth,
Pacific sideband snail, shooting stars, variegated meadowhawk.*

Contents

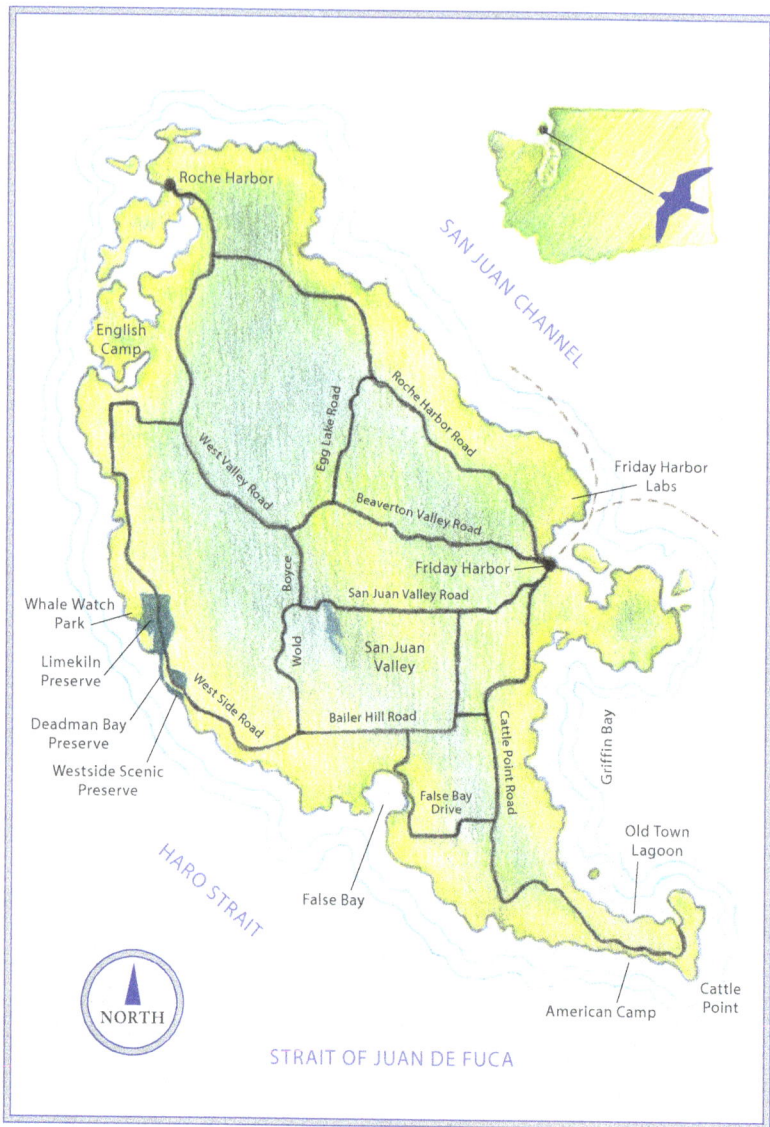

Roche Harbor

SAN JUAN CHANNEL

English Camp

West Valley Road

Egg Lake Road

Roche Harbor Road

Beaverton Valley Road

Friday Harbor Labs

Friday Harbor

Boyce

San Juan Valley Road

Whale Watch Park

Wold

San Juan Valley

Limekiln Preserve

Deadman Bay Preserve

West Side Road

Bailer Hill Road

Cattle Point Road

Griffin Bay

Westside Scenic Preserve

False Bay Drive

Old Town Lagoon

False Bay

HARO STRAIT

NORTH

American Camp

Cattle Point

STRAIT OF JUAN DE FUCA

San Juan Island
Washington State

Islands in the Salish Sea

The San Juan Archipelago, located in the northwest corner of Washington State, is comprised of over 400 islands, rocks and reefs embraced by the Salish Sea. The group boasts 375 miles of shoreline framed by coastal mountain ranges, neighbored by Vancouver's Island, only a short sail from Puget Sound across the Strait of Juan de Fuca, and within easy motor-boating distance to the Gulf Islands of British Columbia and the Canadian mainland.

San Juan, the second largest island, encompasses 55 square miles of green dappled forests, vibrant wildflower-infused prairies and grasslands, constantly evolving dunes and sand-pebbled beaches, and fresh and saltwater wetlands that nudge the ragged edges of the inland sea.

At this convergence of international boundaries, the rocky resting places—ice-sculpted and glacial-scarred long ago—are home to some of the most biologically diverse ecosystems in the world. Within these specialized realms, a fascinating array of plants and animals endure and thrive—each finding its unique niche in the web of life of this sun-infused, wet, wind-blown and rain-shadowed world.

*These are the ancient lands and waters
of the Coast Salish People who have called this
place home since time immemorial. May we honor
and protect inherent, aboriginal, and treaty rights
passed down through the generations.*

Preface

I awakened at first light with birds on my mind. It was September 20, the waning days of fall migration for some birds, and I had been watching all month for Audubon's yellow-rumped warblers to pass through San Juan Island. The little yellow songbirds are a common breeder in coniferous forests and mixed woodlands throughout the West. While some nest on the island, I was waiting for the yellow rumps that bred farther north in Canada and Alaska and streamed down the Pacific Flyway in large flocks past the island on their way south. I had kept track of the spectacular surges for over twenty years always noting their dates of passage in my field journal. It was a thrill to spot those first flocks of late summer warblers in the canopy.

I chose the forest at the Friday Harbor Labs to explore, one of several sites I had been monitoring. I was out of the house, binoculars in hand, by nine o'clock on what promised to be a good day for flying: calm, clear, and temperatures in the mid-60s. A crescent moon hung high in the pale blue sky above Friday Harbor.

I spent the morning walking the Fire Trail through western red cedars and Douglas firs and exploring the rocky shoreline along San Juan Channel. The forest was rife with Pacific madrones just coming into luscious orange and gold fruit the robins favored. Many of the breeding birds had already left the island. I missed the haunting refrain of the Swainson's thrush that had accompanied me on my explorations all summer. Time passed. I regrouped and sat still in the woods by Beaverton Cove watching and waiting for the golden birds while enjoying the chorus of calls from resident towhees, chickadees, nuthatches and wrens. I especially listened for the soft tapping of red-breasted sapsuckers who were predictable September visitors in these woods and, more recently, breeding residents, as well.

By early afternoon, I was disappointed—again—at not finding warblers and about to make it a day. Then, standing near an old pear tree by the Whitely Center, I heard the sound of soft *chek* notes down University Road by the bridge. And soon, more. The yellow rumps were finally here. I rushed toward the call notes in the woods. Looking into the madrones, I could see the birds' familiar forms. They were tiny as tea cups, clad in fall plumage with faint yellow throats and rumps, and a splash of sun on their sides. Their soft, tannish-gray backs were the color of old pine cones still affixed to the ghost trees that leaned toward the nearby bluff by the harbor. The yellow hues mimicked the fading leaves of deciduous trees they would forage through along the Flyway as they continued their journey. The muted coloration enhanced their invisibility to predators.

From a handful of warblers to several dozen, and quickly many more. They kept coming, fluttering into the trees. I clambered down a trail over fallen logs and piles of woody debris to an old Douglas fir that I could lean against to be still, watch and listen to the gathering. Yellow-green light shot through the canopy, streaming into the forest on the dappled birds. They were foraging everywhere: pock-marked snags, pine and cedar boughs, ocean spray with seeds, and a spent juniper offering light green lichen hanging in sheets and full of bugs. Their only sound was a chorus of soft, metallic *cheks* but mostly the birds were putting their energy into foraging and trusting in the integrity of the flock to stay safe.

They flew by, tumbled down through the foliage, and nearly brushed my shoulder too busy to be afraid. The resident birds stayed out of the fray intuiting that this passage was serious business for the warblers. There would be time enough later, after they had gone through, to resume foraging.

More birds appeared. The flock now numbered close to a thousand. I suspected yellow rumps that had nested in this patch of green during the spring and summer might join this band of travelers on the continuing flight south. There is safety in numbers for many migrating birds.

I watched for forty minutes. Mesmerized! Then in an instant, as if on cue, the flock pulled together and streamed out over the harbor in an eruption of urgent wingbeats and away—chattering loudly as they flew off to points south.

There was a gentle joy in my moments with the soft, busy birds. As I stood watching them disappear, a kingfisher took flight and rattled along the shoreline while heron croaked a cranky admonition for the disturbance from the beach below. Chartreuse light still filtered through the tree tops. This woodland had done its job for the travelers. For the time being, all seemed right in this world.

~

Those forty minutes I stood in the forest and watched the warblers were exhilarating. It was nothing unusual for the yellow rumps but unforgettable to me. I was reminded how important that small patch of woodland was to the beautiful birds' survival on their journeys south. And how other dramatic occurrences, larger than life events and small wonders, were played out on the island every day.

I was lured to San Juan Island on the far western shores of Washington State by its natural beauty and a career opportunity. I have stayed for over thirty years as the director of a small natural history museum, land steward, co-founder of the San Juan Nature

Institute, surveyor of swans, captive breeding specialist for an endangered butterfly and nature writer. I found home. As a naturalist, exploring the woods, beaches, wetlands, prairies and in-betweens is second nature. I find beauty at every turn in the trail. I have seen the complexity in the lives of some animals and the simplicity in others. Questions answered and mysteries left unsolved.

The island has stories to tell. By observing closely, I have seen how the flora and fauna flow together into a magnificent whole. Each species has something unique to show us about this place. And, always, I have been humbled by the impermanence of it all.

In my first book, *Rainshadow World*, I wrote about killer whales, bald eagles, trumpeter swans and red fox, among others, the highly visible animals that captivate both islanders and visitors. In this work, the stories are about some of the lesser-known species of San Juan Island—those beating wild hearts that go largely unnoticed. These are the keepers of the web of life in one of the most beautiful Pacific Northwest settings.

My accounts are based upon what I do best: sitting still in the grass along a split rail fence watching short-eared owls making a living on the prairie; following tailed blue butterflies through their short adult lives among the beach peas at American Camp; or spending an afternoon with an off course shorebird that stopped over at a saltwater lagoon to rest while making its way home.

The stories all take place in the terrestrial ecosystem of San Juan Island: a vireo nesting in a mixed woodland; a moth living its short life on vegetated dunes; or western bluebirds defying the odds and returning to their native range after a decades-long absence. And, they are arranged seasonally—exploring an island year—for continuity.

There are nods to island history, as well, for to truly know a place one needs to understand what has come before. The photographs— save three—were taken at the time of the event or soon thereafter.

Yes, the short-eared owl on the cover is the same bird that "ruffled its feathers" at me along Redoubt Road.

The Nature of this small island in the Salish Sea is remarkable to behold. It is also fragile. I bear witness here solely to the existence of these lives. Why they matter is my truth, nothing more. Yet, underscoring the connectedness of all living things has its place here, too, and reflects the purpose of this book. It is that slender thread of continuity between us and them that forms the bonds that ensure we will continue to take care of this rich realm, of its wildlife, and of ourselves.

This is what I saw. Isn't it beautiful! The rest is up to you.

AUTHOR'S NOTE: Throughout the text, I have used the vernacular names of flora and fauna. For some plants, I included also the scientific names by which they are commonly regarded. These names have been set in lower case to enhance readability.

Vernacular names of plants vary, sometimes significantly, from source to source. I have used Pojar & MacKinnon's *Plants of the Pacific Northwest Coast*, Kozloff's *Plants of Western Oregon, Washington & British Columbia*, and his earlier work *Plants and Animals of the Pacific Northwest* as my references.

The AOS *Checklist of North and Middle American Birds* and *Butterflies of the Pacific Northwest* by Pyle & LaBar were references for bird and butterfly names.

The University of Washington Friday Harbor Marine Laboratories, in the text, is called "The Labs," a common term of reference by islanders, Lab affiliates and friends.

American Camp is a unit of the San Juan Island National Historical Park. Limekiln Preserve is located adjacent to Lime Kiln Point State Park owned and managed by the San Juan County Conservation Land Bank. The Cattle Point locations are part of the San Juan Islands National Monument properties managed by the U.S. Bureau of Land Management.

1

SITTING STILL WITH TWILIGHT OWLS

The vernal equinox was at hand. This short-eared owl would soon be leaving for its nesting grounds after a winter residency on the American Camp prairie.

A buffy-brown bird with bright spangles on its back and radiant yellow eyes rose like an apparition over the ridge from South Beach—a raptor making its living on San Juan Island. It was coming my way flying low over a grassland pockmarked with rabbit warrens, a red fox den and disarray of bracken ferns that had long ago overrun lush meadows of camas that shone bedazzled blue beside the Salish Sea.

The bird was a short-eared owl—a familiar winter visitor to the south end of the island. On its daily rounds, the owl covered a lot of territory from the dunes at Cattle Point, across Finlayson Ridge, over to July Beach and throughout the open spaces of American Camp. The twilight hours seemed especially productive for this resourceful predator and thus the term "twilight owl" coined long ago.

I was admiring its form: a stout, medium-sized owl with a strong, steady wingbeat. Three or four flaps, then an effortless glide sent it floating over the scruffy plain. It held its broad, slightly bowed, round-tipped wings outstretched to nearly four feet cruising the gentle breeze with casual ease. Dark, comma-like markings at its wrists were prominent identifiers.

The striking bird was hunting—its wide-eyed gaze fixed mindfully on the canvas of grass. Those keen gold eyes, encircled in black, were deeply set in its tawny, flat face. A short-feathered ruff rimmed bright white brows, lores and chin. Owl wore an expression more of surprise than of menace.

Owl worked its way upslope adjacent to Pickett's Lane, hovered momentarily over an especially dense patch of grass watching and listening for unsuspecting prey in the tangle of winter-weary vegetation. Then a wheelabout and feetfirst pounce into the turf and, coming up empty, retreating to the split rail fence to regroup. Owl preened its cream-feathered legs, did a full-body shake to settle flight feathers, then combed those plumes with a short, black beak. It perched for several minutes facing south.

The short-eared owl watched and waited, keying on the dune grass across the road occasionally turning its head from side to side wary of intruders, perhaps. Soon, a silent liftoff, a sweep low over the grass down the fence line, another short hover, then a dismissive turnabout and gone over the dunes.

～

It was two days past the vernal equinox. After a morning of deep chill and stiff wind the tempo of the day changed. The temperature nudged into the 50s, and the unexpected warmth beckoned me to the park. My goal was to get one last look at short-eared owls before they left for their breeding grounds to the north and east.

Historically, this grassland was defined as prairie, strewn with the remnants of an ages-old glacial presence. Granite boulders splashed with light green, orange and yellow lichen stood like sentinels across a landscape rich with stories that shaped the character of a once wild place transitioning to twenty-first century realities. The area was flush with birds of prey: bald and golden eagles, peregrine falcons, red-tailed and rough-legged hawks, northern harriers, kestrels, short-eared owls, great horned owls and others feasted on the small mammals that scurried about the tall grass on the plain. What a great spot for birding.

I had been watching short-eared owls for many years and, while not common on the island, I knew where and when to find them. American Camp was their place and mine. The spunky owls had been successfully sourcing the grasslands for decades.

As a birder, I found the owls were especially fun to watch. One may catch only a glimpse of a favored species in the field: a nondescript grebe diving far offshore; a raptor soaring high overhead; or a warbler flitting through the canopy. But, as an open country bird, short-eared owls are highly visible, animated, often found in pairs, and likely to hunt in the same area repeatedly and for extended periods of time. And they are beautiful to behold.

Encountering the owls—some call them shorties—immediately upon entering the park was an excellent start to the afternoon. Their presence was unpredictable but an early sighting usually meant there are more encounters to come—with a little patience. I circled back off Pickett's Lane, and onto a pot-holed access road that led to Robert's Redoubt and the Parade Grounds at the historic park. Split rail fencing brought order where hundreds and thousands of years ago wolves roamed, Indigenous people hunted and gathered, and Nature was still the dominating force of life.

Proceeding slowly northward up the way, I spotted another owl. This was going to be fun. I parked the car by the Redoubt, found a stretch of split rail fence I could lean against, and settled into the tall grass. The plan was to sit still, be invisible, and spend some time with the owls without disturbing their space or activity.

Marsh owl, swamp owl, prairie owl were all early names for the short-eared owl. Standing a little over a foot tall, this day-flying raptor is a superb example of form and function.   Plumes of rich brown, buff and white mottling, with streaky breasts, blend seamlessly into the tall grass. Soft plumage and the comb-like leading edge of the primary feathers and fringed trailing feathers reduce turbulence giving them agile flight in sometimes windy conditions

Their ears are set asymmetrically on their stout heads so they can locate prey in both horizontal and vertical plains simultaneously detecting even the subtlest movement of mice or voles in the grass. The feathered tufts on its head, while giving the appearance of ears (and thus its name), are actually display feathers only.

The length of the short-eared owl's winter stay on the island is predicated upon the population of these small mammals. In lean years, the owls come and go quickly. In years such as this one, they may stay all winter. They seem gregarious by nature, sometimes hunting in pairs or small loose flocks.

I was barely settled when I spotted the owl again. It was working its way south on a slow prowl below the Redoubt scanning the prairie grass with its laser vision from about thirty feet. Occasionally, it would wheel down to grasp a white-footed deer mouse or Townsend's vole still numerous on the plain. I couldn't see the tiny creatures scurrying in the grass and hiding in the tangle of winter vines, but I knew they were there. So did Owl. After one missed opportunity, it lifted out of the grass with four floppy wingbeats and coasted low to a fencepost for a perch.

It is a luxury to watch owls in the afternoon. This day-flying species is a specialist at hunting in low light, too, often active at dawn and dusk. On San Juan, they hunt at last light cruising the ridge above South Beach as the sun sets on the inland sea in magnificent hues of yellow, scarlet and gold. Twilight owl, indeed!

Soon, another owl appeared in a slow glide down the hill from the Redoubt. It joined its kin in a series of aerial wheeling, twists and turns that I imagined only slightly rippled the warm air. I could hear the duo exchanging soft chirps and barks and suspected the interaction was part of a bonding and mating ritual. Some call it a sky dance. Males and females are similar in plumage (females slightly larger and darker than males) but without seeing the signature talon grasps and wing clapping I was not certain if this was a breeding pair. Their aerial acrobatics were an impressive choreography of life if still some time and distance away from spring nesting possibly in fallow fields and prairie remnants in eastern Washington and beyond.

The sky dance continued with flourishes. Then, a female northern harrier appeared, meandering up the slope from Grandma's Cove. She flew on long, wide wings, with a similar flap and glide wingbeat as the owls. The hawk's cinnamon breast feathers glistened as she tilted and weaved in the afternoon light. Her white rump gleaming behind folds of bronze feathers on her back gave Hawk's identity away. She spotted the owls.

The harrier climbed the air to get a better view, gazed at the duo through earnest golden eyes, pumped her wings several times and turned in their direction. The owls saw her coming and broke off their dance. One swiftly retreated upslope. The other sped straightaway at the hawk shouting a harsher version of the barking chants I had heard earlier. It was a gutsy move by Owl. The hawk was a bigger bird. It was soon rebuked, though, and veered off toward Old Town Lagoon. The owl duo went their separate ways.

The short-eared owls soon reconnected and, for over two hours, hunted, parried with the harrier, continued their barking chats to one another, and perched on boulders and fence rails to rest and consider their options. I admired their command of the grassland—undaunted by the harrier. It must have been a good year for voles that encouraged their stay.

Watching the hawk and the owls—both species perfectly plumed to range the prairie—was like witnessing a master class in hunting technique. While diverse in form, these birds functioned in similar ways, using keen eyesight and hearing, hover hunting, and agility to great advantage. There was tension in the air, but they managed to coexist—if not always peacefully—in this rich golden plain.

$\sim$

Suddenly the owls departed over the ridge toward Griffin Bay. I did not see what caused the swift retreat, perhaps the flyby of a peregrine falcon, but their absence gave me time to ponder this winter world. I wondered when the owls first appeared at this place that began, eons ago, as a rough-hewn plain bound by plate tectonics to the western margin of North America. Much later, the landscape was sculpted by massive sheets of ice during the Fraser Glaciation, habituated by the Coast Salish with their sophisticated hunting and gathering culture, and changed again with the arrival of Europeans and the development of Belle Vue Sheep Farm by the Hudson's Bay Company on this very spot.

The Pig War (1859-72) politicized the plain. The Homestead Act of 1882 brought domestication as agriculture had its hay day. Land use transformed it again into a military reservation until 1923. A large condominium development along these grassy slopes was thwarted in the 1960s. Finally, San Juan Island National Historical Park was designated in 1966. Looking back at the history of this relatively small patch of land reminded me of the likely challenges any species of wildlife faced as the culture, use and significance of their habitat changed.

Local ornithologist Mark Lewis documented short-eared owls at American Camp in March of 1984 and islander Richard Wright in June of 1985. It is likely the owls had been at least migrants through the islands, if not breeding residents, for some time by then.

As I waited for the owls to reappear, I listened for the first spring song of ground-nesting savannah sparrows. They were due to arrive back to San Juan any day from their winter retreat to the south. No thin, reedy calls were emitted from the grass by the slight, brown birds with the bright yellow lores but I knew their familiar melody would be floating over the plain soon or perhaps they were already home and just out of earshot. And with luck, the vesper sparrow's soft, unassuming song would be returning, too. While not as abundant as the savannah, the vespers were still holding tenuously to their claim of small grassy niches at the south end.

Anticipating the savannahs reminded me of times gone by when I sat in this same spot listening for the ebullient reverie of the Eurasian skylark that once called this place home. When I moved to the island in the mid-1980s, skylarks were still breeders here, having made their place on San Juan presumably as migrants from across Haro Strait on Vancouver Island where they had been introduced in 1903. Lewis and Sharpe reported that they were first sighted on San Juan in 1960 and nested here ten years later. After the turn into 2000, the bird's presence here declined due to factors still being debated including an increasing rabbit population that decimated their grassland nesting sites.

I found the original documentation of that first sighting in an online archive: August 15, 1960. James A. Bruce sighted the skylark while walking along the prairie at what we now call American Camp. He appeared to have flushed the "brown bird" out of the grass and noted its unfamiliar call as it flew up and away. Its white outer tail feathers, crest and short tail were diagnostic, as was a flight pattern that brought the bird sharply back down into the grass a short distance away. Bruce described the terrain as "rolling sheep pasture" inhabited by western meadowlarks and savannah sparrows. He mused that Haro Strait, adjacent to the grassland at the south end of the island, appeared to have been an "effective barrier" in preventing large-scale migration of the skylark from Vancouver Island, B.C. several miles west.

Bruce's comment about the presence of meadowlarks in August was especially interesting. Lewis and Sharpe noted the larks as common breeders on the island until, at least, 1960. Now they are fall and winter residents only on the island.

The arrival of the skylark in North America was pondered by one of our earliest nature writers, Susan Fenimore Cooper, who wrote with enthusiasm in *Rural Hours* from New York state in 1850 about the possibility of both the European skylark and the nightingale being introduced to America. Fenimore Cooper thought the skylark's song would: "… indeed form a charming addition to our native choir …" Attempts were made in New Jersey to accomplish such a feat in the early 1900s, but faltered. Alas, it was not to be. The San Juans remained the only breeding population in the contiguous U.S. until their disappearance here around 2000. Its numbers in North America never surpassed one thousand birds.

It has been many years since I heard the skylark's song—a string of nearly endless rapid-fire warbles and chips rising out of the grass along Pickett's Lane. Birding the south end of the island often included checking on the larks, usually in early morning when the light rose with their cheerful song. My last journal entry was 6 March 1998 from Pickett's Lane where I wrote: "Was that a Skylark I heard?" Looking back, it was a poignant entry. I wish I had not taken the presence of that beautiful songster for granted and stayed a spell longer to listen to its song. Sadly, now I know how it sounds when the skylarks stop singing. Their disappearance is a loss to the soul of this piece of grassland along the inland sea.

Soon the owls returned and resumed hunting. As sharp-edged shadows gathered by the Redoubt, the predators followed the light to the east. I read in the classic *Birds of America* (1917) that short-eared owls are rather stupid. Really? As dusk approached, a mature bald eagle cruised by and I saw the prairie owls dive for cover in the tall grass. That seemed like a smart move to me.

It was obvious that *Asio flammeus* preferred their privacy and were reluctant to hunt close by if I stood in the open. I retreated to my car and admired these shy souls from afar: their dexterity, feisty chanting barks, and preference for perching on the rabbit-proof fence as a vantage point for hunting. And I noted the sun leaving sparkling pools of silver light on Haro Strait and clouds parting to reveal the snow-capped peaks of the Olympic Mountains on the peninsula. A closer encounter with the owls would have been nice but it was enough to simply sit a spell and watch them leading their intriguing lives from a distance.

The sun continued its slow western descent as a sense of peace settled over the prairie. A red fox leisurely crossed the road and continued along its well-trodden trail. Western meadowlarks ceased their chorus of bubbly chatter that had been background music to the afternoon's events. Soon, they would be leaving too, perhaps going only as far as eastern Washington to breed. The light was fading. I lost sight of the pair. It was nearly time to go and I got out of the car for a final scan.

As I walked toward the fence line, one of the owls flew in from the east just off my shoulder and perched on a split rail fifteen feet away. It was facing the setting sun. The feathers on its back shone like those silver spangles in the lingering light. The sorcerer turned its head and looked at me with a penetrating gaze, blinked its golden eyes, and turned back to the sun. I held my breath. It glanced back a second time, shook its feathers hard, then lifted off the fence and was fifty yards away before I remembered to breathe. The short-eared owl dipped once gently into the grass before it disappeared. It was not curiosity that prompted Owl's flyby but rather a statement that, even from my considerable distance, I had stayed too long in its territory. I had "ruffled its feathers" and it was time to go.

2

SALISH BLUES

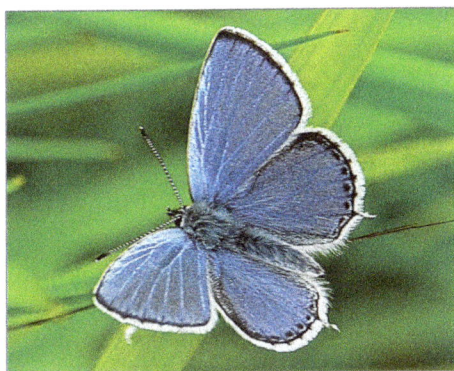

*A western tailed blue perched
in the grass on the backshore—
one of the earliest butterflies to
emerge for an island spring. Its
short life was filled with perils
and expectations.*

She caught my eye fluttering about the beach pea among a jumble of driftwood and shifting sand—the tiniest of butterflies about the size of my thumbnail. It was a western tailed blue and I was thrilled to see her. Gray skies had turned to Salish blue and how better to celebrate spring than to quest for blue butterflies.

I had already found several early blue wildflowers: common camas at Westside Preserve, blue-eyed Mary at The Labs, and just a hint of seashore lupine along the Lighthouse Trail at Cattle Point. While checking on the blue and white blooms of *Lupinus littoralis*, I caught a glimpse of two echo azure butterflies in the willow thicket behind the dunes. They were waiting out an energetic breeze. But I was looking for an old friend and knew just where to go. So, on to South Beach and the western tailed blues.

I drove down Pickett's Lane with butterflies on my mind and parked at an area near the shore. As I was getting out of the car, I spied a blue streak landing on a picnic table by the beach. A quick glance through my binoculars brought a start. It was not a butterfly. It was a mountain bluebird stopping by the island on its migration to breeding grounds farther north. What great luck.

Bluebirds, while not common in the San Juans, are not rare. In the 1960s, western bluebirds were breeders here, then vanished; only recently have they made a recovery via a successful reintroduction program.

Mountain bluebirds are regarded as migrants, not breeding residents, of our island group. I had seen them before. Years ago, a female mountain bluebird at Mt. Finlayson had left an indelible impression—a fine fall day made perfect by its appearance, perched on a lichen-covered glacial erratic at the Jackson Vista Point overlooking Haro Strait. That bird stayed in the area for several days, never straying far from Finlayson, until it resumed its journey.

Now, with perseverance, I can find mountain bluebirds either during spring or fall migration at Finlayson or American Camp. This blue—a female—was using the picnic table and nearby drift for perch hunting: dropping into the grass, snatching insects, and returning to her rest. She continued this feeding strategy for several minutes. I could clearly see the ripples in the soft gray plumes on her crown, back, and breast, and a light hue of powder blue that washed over the thrush's wings and etched all but the gray tip of her tail. What a beautiful bird!

What a dilemma! Stay with the bluebird or carry on to the tailed blues? I opted for the butterfly and reluctantly moved on, hoping I would encounter the "little blue herald" again.

There is a predictable succession of plant blooms that forecast butterfly emergence on this stretch of backbeach. Tiny redstem filaree and pinkish dove-foot geranium bloom, as do carpets of crisp white teesdalia and western buttercups; patches of lustrous field chickweed fill out the gathering. Echo azures and silvery blue butterflies emerge to the beckoning of these plants and to warming air rising off the sand and Salish Sea. From a nearby nettle thicket, ornate satyr anglewings cruise over dune grass while an occasional mourning cloak or Milbert's tortoiseshell flutters over the willows at the spring just off Salmon Bank Road near Alaska Packer Rock.

It takes one more indispensable plant to coax the tailed blues out of their winter slumber along this strand of backbeach—the flowering of beach pea (*Lathyrus japonicus*), their host plant. These sea peas of coastal dunes are pale pink to purplish-blue in bloom, arranged in loose clusters on vines of six to twelve inches and slightly succulent green leaves. They trail, creep and climb over other plants keeping low to the ground. The rhizomes of this plant run deep, which helps stabilize the sand.

I walked the sandy substrate between the driftwood line and the backbeach. The peas were in bloom and, from the looks of it, had been for several days. That was good news as it meant there should be several tailed blues flying.

Then, yes!! There was the grail—that little gossamer-winged beauty fluttering from pea blossom to pea vine and all about the drift and shore. And then another. The male was crisp and boldly blue above with dark margins and whitish beneath. When he folded his wings, the butterfly took on a silvery sheen that made him nearly invisible among the foliage. The second was a female, more discrete in coloration, a modest brownish-blue above that likely helped camouflage her from predators.

I watched the pair from several feet away using binoculars, the only means to truly appreciate the subtleties of the scaling on their wings. Light played on the dorsal surface transforming the color of the female from slaty-brownish/gray to a brighter blue as the angle of the light changed.

I spent about two hours among the tailed blues that afternoon, being careful not to crush the beach pea blooms. They continued to flutter on those purplish-blue wings just above the low-slung peas entwined with grasses and lupine that perfectly hide their frail blue frames along the shore.

The blues investigated every niche, alighting on the peas, on pieces of drift, in the sand, and on small erratics. They never stayed for long. A female perched on a narrow, green leaf of beach grass, wings open, then folded, and performed a pirouette on the blade to catch the best angle of the sun for a short bask. Then, off she fluttered. They dodged and weaved to avoid the sand wasps stopping at tiny forget-me-nots and the yellow blooms of curvaceous small-flowered fiddleneck. Over the dunes. Over the drift. Fluttering enthusiastically, then back to the peas dipping that long, unfurled proboscis into the purple blooms for a sweet taste of nectar. And finally, time for a short mating dance on the beach grass and a successful coming together. It was a joyous way to celebrate spring.

As my field season surveying island marble butterflies was about to begin, I reluctantly left the tailed blues with the promise to return. I knew it might be a while.

Soon, it was June. I had lost track of time in the dunes releasing adult island marbles I had captive-reared. The marbles' life cycle took a year to complete. I had raised their eggs and larvae from the previous June, watched the fifth instars (caterpillars) pupate into chrysalids, and monitored their slumber in my lab (under contract with the Park Service) all winter. Being responsible for such a rare butterfly found only in the San Juan Islands had been a nerve-wracking process. Finally watching several dozen successfully emerge from those chrysalids and returning them to the dunes to fly free had been a great experience. It had also monopolized my time. Summer solstice jolted me back to reality. I knew the blue's season was on the wane. I headed for the backshore hoping I was not too late to see them one more time.

The scene had changed dramatically. The beach pea was waning. I knew *L. japonicas* was near the end of its bloom. Once the plant developed its fruit (elongated brown pods) the tailed blues' flight season at the backbeach would end, as well. There was only a small window left to enjoy the blues.

It was late afternoon. I headed for my favorite vantage point just back from the driftwood line and settled on the sand surrounded by beach grass, yellow sand-verbena and the scarlet inflorescence of sheep sorrel that made portions of the backbeach glow red.

A breeze was blowing in from the west. I knew the butterflies would soon seek refuge from the chill. Maybe I would find them retiring for the night.

At the height of the western tailed blue's flight season here, dozens of the demure butterflies may be found among the lush peas growing over long stretches of the backshore. Now, so late in the season, most of them had lived out their butterfly lives. They only survived as flying adults—at best—two weeks but more likely only a few days.

Luckily, I was not too late. I found a few pea-loving blues, their fleeting wingbeats taking them to and fro the margins of the beach. The blue I finally keyed upon appeared to be an old female although it was hard to tell even with good glass. Her wings had faded to a light powder blue with a brownish-gray cast. There were nicks, scars and tears along the margins of her wings. At least one of the "tails" (hair-like protrusions at the bottom of the wings) had worn away. I strained to find the orange lunule: a crescent-shaped marking that adorns the hindwings of most

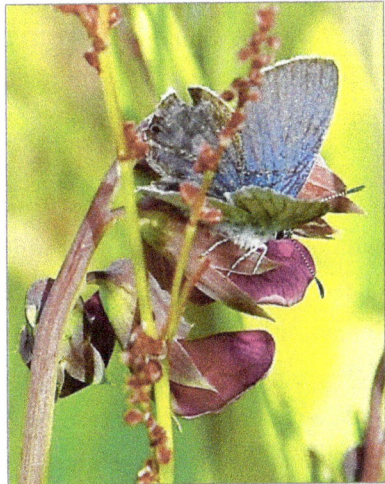

The old tailed blue on beach pea.

tailed blues. Having seen many old butterflies, it was clear this one had endured challenges including bird strikes, wind and harsh weather. It had not been an altogether welcoming spring for butterflies.

Possibly a week or so before, this tailed blue may have emerged from her chrysalis in the sandy beach pea realm as an adult butterfly. She found a mate almost immediately; reproduction was her imperative. Once the coupling had occurred, the blooming peas beckoned her with nectar and a platform for depositing her eggs. The blues' life cycle was a true metamorphosis that took nearly a year. Once breeding and egg laying were accomplished, the blues remaining challenge was simply to survive. Judging from the multi-layered habitat of predatory insects and birds, threats from the hiker's boot and other human interventions, plus rain and windstorms, I found it miraculous this little blue butterfly survived to old age.

I sat for a long time watching *Cupido amyntula*. The chill was descending. She was slowing down. I contemplated her moves and took in the scene. Nearby, a piece of driftwood had been turned into some creature's dining table strewn with half-opened and remnant beach pea pods. Ants, spiders, black-and-white wasps and tiny four-legged green beings were scurrying about the substrate. Feathers blew by. A maze of tiny trails through the vegetation spoke to the presence of voles or mice in the area. They all had roles to play in this niche.

The old blue butterfly positioned and repositioned herself as the wind brushed through the latticework of pea vines, grasses and sheep sorrel that surrounded it. An orange-striped bumblebee flew in and dislodged the fragile insect from high on one late-blooming flower sending her into the grass. She folded her wings and tried settling in, but it did not seem to be the right spot. The blue fluttered just a bit out of the grass, then back onto a blooming pea. She closed her wings tightly again and swayed to the rhythm of the sea breeze. The faint chips of juvenile savannah sparrows, the bold pronouncements of white-crowned sparrows, and the buzzing of more fat bumblebees dispelled the quiet of the drift as the sun slid toward the horizon behind Vancouver Island.

It was a beautiful scene. I looked about and saw two more blues disappear into the blue-green maze of beach peas and grass. Their frail frames were perfectly camouflaged among the sand and drift. They had survived another day.

Sitting quietly along the drift and observing the steadfast tailed blue settling in for one of her last nights on the backshore was a poignant event. Her end time was near. The old butterfly repositioned herself again, folded her wings tightly, and was still. The desolate drifts and dunes had served the blue well. I felt gratitude for sharing those moments with the western tailed blue. It was a view into her life few visitors to this beach would even imagine. It was hard to leave the beautiful butterfly—a symbol of life's enduring ways—but I finally wished her well and walked back down the shore. I was already looking forward to seeing her kin—next year's new generation of spring blues.

3
VIREO SPRING

In May, a Cassin's vireo settled on her nest of twigs, lichens, cattail down and spider's silk at Limekiln Preserve. The next generation of forest dwellers was on the way.

Zeedle, zeedle, zeedle, zeet-chee. "Oh, there's a black-throated gray," I exclaimed. Good start! My morning walk with long-time birding pal Jean Shreve held promise. We were looking for warblers—a spring ritual. That high-spirited, buzzy birdcall with the upturned note at the end told us it was going to be a happy day.

The path through the forest at Limekiln Preserve was scattered with the spent flowers of Pacific madrone—tiny, white, urn-shaped orbs that lent lightness to the trail. Near the end of April, the mixed woodland of cedars, firs, maples and alders glowed in shades of green, gold and chartreuse. The air was still brisk but soft. It was full on spring.

We noted the last of Calypso, the island's most intriguing orchid, and the coming of spotted coralroot and woodland starflower emerging from the duff. Robins chortled, an orange-crowned warbler softly trilled, and a varied thrush's harmonic call wafted through the trees. We rounded a bend in the trail, scrambled up a steep, rocky incline and emerged in a clearing that looked out over a densely vegetated slope of big-leaf maples that rose to the ridge of Mount Dallas. We stopped to scan for birds and simultaneously pointed excitedly to a nest in a madrone downslope from the path.

It was a tiny, woven cup of twigs, leaves, fibers, lichen, spider silk and cattail down suspended from the crook in a spindly branch of the arbutus. The frame of the vessel was adorned with flower petals and spider egg cases. Overhead, a tangle of contorted limbs and greenery offered cover and camouflage for the nursery.

What seemed a precarious perch was a sturdy structure testimony to the wonder of animal architecture. Jean and I thought at first it might be a hummingbird's nest. Then we spied a little gray-headed bird with a white throat sitting motionless in the basket of (presumed) eggs peering over the rim at us through sparkling, dark brown eyes. No, it was not a hummingbird, but we weren't sure of its identity. I used a long lens to take a photo then quickly retreated to avoid disturbing the nest's tranquility. What a great find! And a mystery to solve later. We cheerfully went on our way literally giggling with delight.

Later, I took to books to identify the little forester—likely a Cassin's vireo, one of four vireo species found in the San Juans.

There are two conspicuous identifiers for this vireo: its white spectacles and its song. The male Cassin's sings incessantly in the woods adding to the chorus of nuthatches, chickadees, juncos, robins, thrushes, flycatchers and others that form the sylvan bird community. The song has been described as a series of burry, whistled phrases with sharp, rising and falling inflections. It suggests to me a tiny, spectacled bird with an air of self-confidence. Endlessly singing—sometimes almost rambling—as it flits through the canopy. I find the melody a happy addition to any walk in Lime Kiln Woods.

Ornithologist William Dawson elaborated: "Cassin sings as he works; and, as he works a good deal of the time, albeit in leisurely fashion, he sings in tiny phrases, separated by unembarrassed intervals of silence, a sort of soliloquizing commentary on life, very pleasant to the ear."

My photo of the bird was inconclusive. I needed a closer look at those spectacles and to hear its song. So, it was back down the green corridors of West Side Road the next morning to take another look. As I got out of my car at the turnout, the spirited strains of the vireo were echoing through the trees. Unmistakable. Good! Now, to see those white spectacles.

The morning sun shone through the celadon leaves of the maples as I headed for the nest. One of the parents was perched silently high in the cup. This time I could see its white spectacles. Yes, it was a Cassin's. The small North American songbird ranges from southern British Columbia through the western coastal United States to southern Mexico where it overwinters.

I settled carefully into the shadows nearby to watch for the mate. Both parents participate in brooding eggs and raising offspring. The vocal male would arrive soon-—I hoped. An hour went by. I listened to woodpeckers drumming, warblers warbling, and bees buzzing. No vireo. The sun rose over the ridge of Mount Dallas to the east and shone directly on the nest. The female adjusted her position by rising slightly to take full advantage of the warmth. Huge big-leaf maples that shared the slopes with the madrones and alders were in full pendulous bloom. Their flowers adding a yellow-gold luster to the air.

I moved down slope to investigate wildflowers, clambering over erratics that had been deposited there during the final withdrawal of the Fraser Glaciation 13,000 years ago. The enormous, moss-covered rocks were nurseries, too, festooned with newly emerging, yet rock-hugging stonecrop whose succulent silvery-gray-green leaves showed off tiny yellow flowers that brightened the forest. This woodland had undergone many transitions since that monumental ice age event. I wondered when the first vireos found this forest— long before the First People arrived, I suspected.

My forest watch for the vireo continued. Finally, I saw the male flitting purposefully through layers of green leaves. He started to sing. This was no accidental song, rather a full-throated, vigorous reverie intended to impress. He paused in a madrone close to the nest and poured out wild notes with a halting cadence. The breeze picked up the melody and escorted it through the trees.

Then, the parental switch at the nursery. In an instant, the male dropped down to the nest tree and hesitated only a moment on the natal bough while the female flew out and away. He quickly settled over the creamy white and speckled eggs for his turn at incubation. All was well. I retreated, satisfied at having witnessed the small but vitally important element of the pair's egg brooding routine.

~

The vireo remained on my mind as I continued my rounds at Lime Kiln. The drama of the nest was unfolding along the shoreline of Westside Lake—an eight-acre gem of fresh, deep water surrounded by a riot of cattails, rushes, sedges, black twinberry and red-osier dogwood. It was an idyllic setting with the seasonal chorus of red-winged blackbirds and newly arrived warblers.

Westside Lake was excavated in the 1970s by a local developer as an amenity to his proposed waterfront housing development adjacent to Haro Strait. Buck's Pond became a reality but through the efforts of preservation-minded islanders, in 1984 the upland property became the site of 36-acre Lime Kiln Point State Park instead. In 1997, an additional 174-acres—Limekiln Preserve— were acquired by the San Juan County Land Bank. This included two-thirds of Buck's Pond renamed Westside Lake. Now, with the addition of adjacent Deadman Bay Preserve and Westside Preserve, there are over 200-acres of shoreline, woodland, wet-lands and freshwater lake for wildlife to utilize and visitors to explore.

Local birders knew Westside Lake as an overwintering site for waterfowl: trumpeter swans, common mergansers, red-breasted mergansers, ring-necked ducks, lesser scaups, green-winged teal and others enjoyed the winter solitude there. Belted kingfishers found carp good fishing. Bald eagles, turkey vultures and hawks soared overhead. My favorite was the pied-billed grebe, a chunky little brown water bird that floated in the shallows, submerged like a submarine to fish, and emitted a bold, hollow, some say cuckoo-like hooting *cuck, cuck, cuck* call during mating season. An endearing quality of the female was carrying her young chicks—splendid in black and white striped faces and red bills—on her back as she navigated the nearshore.

I finished my walk at a rustic bird blind tucked among red cedars and maples along the shore. Island neighbors and friends who have long cherished this spot finely crafted the little shelter. I watched a bright yellow Wilson's warbler, identified by black cap and shining dark eyes, flit from branch to branch along the variegated edge of the lake. It did not make a sound pecking through the green and gold leaves not much smaller than itself. It kept its own counsel in the shadows of a massive moss-laden fir riddled with woodpecker holes, then was gone.

A little before four o'clock, I retreated to the Land Bank parking lot to regroup and sip Pellegrino. At the road edge, a rufous hummingbird was plucking cattail down for her nest. Across the lake, a pair of wood ducks foraged at the water's edge. The female was discreet in rich brown and gray feathering with distinctive white teardrops and subtle blue scapulas while the flamboyant male seemed to flaunt his bright green and purple helmet and flourish of chestnut, black, white and tan plumes. He was a show-off for sure. That was the point.

I listened to the subdued trills of an orange-crowned warbler and the bold pronouncements of olive-sided flycatchers' "quick three beers" call. A pair of Canada geese escorted six tiny goslings—single file—toward the south end of the lake. Scanning the little willow island across the way, I heard the soft, whistled song of yellow-rumped warblers. The Pacific willows were in perfect bloom; their three-inch elongated catkins (flowers) were pale yellow against its rich green lance-shaped leaves and looked a bit like tiny, soft bristle brushes. The catkins were being picked through for insects by the foraging warblers. The birds were nearly invisible in the foliage: gray as the bark of the tree with sunny rumps, throats, and sides. Exquisite!

I stayed for several minutes captivated by a chorus of yellow blooms and birds: the pendulous blossoms of the big-leaf maples, the lemony willow catkins, the twinberries' tiny trumpet-shaped flowers, yellow goslings, goldfinch and Wilson's warbler. Even the tiny black bumblebees had yellow strips.

Then, at the top of the tallest willow, a final striking image caught my eye. A vibrant yellow songbird gleaned in the catkins, perch hunting for bugs. Its lemony head, breast, rump and wing bars were all clues to its identity. It silently flung itself from branch to branch. Bold. Assured. I was hesitant of an identification until I heard the strong, piercing three-syllable *pit-er-ick* call of the male close-by. It was a female western tanager. The male was a bolder-plumaged bird: bright yellow body and shoulders, orange-red head, black wings, and white wing bar. Some characterize its coloring as resembling a flame. I did not see tanagers often, and this sighting made my day.

Twenty more minutes sped by. The day was winding down but there was one more color scheme to admire. The sky was the color of the tiny Veronica blue speedwell wildflowers at my feet, and an echo azure butterfly fluttered about to complete the blue palette. I left in perfect harmony with this spring afternoon.

~

It was some time before I returned to see the vireos. I did not want to disturb them or draw attention to the nest so close to the trail. I worked out the math from that initial visit on April 26. Incubation of the eggs would take twelve to fourteen days, bringing a hatch around May 4 or 5. Then another two weeks for the chicks to fledge.

Curiosity finally prevailed. I returned to the patch of old woods on May 10. There were three chicks in the nest. An adult was nearby with a beak full of grubs. I backed down trail to watch from afar. The vireo flew in, fed the youngsters, and quickly departed. And so did I.

I returned again on May 12 and May 14. All appeared well. The chicks were donned in warm gray garb perfectly camouflaged in the nest. Their mouths gaped yellow—a welcoming receptacle for another meal. There was always loud vocalization from the adults when I appeared. An admonition perhaps. Fair enough. I never got close or stayed long.

I knew it was time for fledging but I did not make it across island to the nest on May 15. When I returned on the 16th, the cup was empty. I waited a few minutes in the hope of hearing the family call in the woods but it was not to be. I assumed the best—successful first flights—and voiced a "good luck and take care" farewell to the birds as I walked away along the trail now occasionally edged with our native wild rose (*Rosa gymnocarpa*). It was smaller than the Nootka, but pleasing for its shy, diminutive stance and soft pink luster. Even the blooming wildflowers were moving on.

What a fine family of vireos! My first close encounter with the beautiful birds. It would have made a better story, I suppose, if I had seen the nestlings fledge, but I did not. I saw enough, though. It was a gift to have watched the adults tend the nest with such care and exuberance.

What does it matter—this pair of little olive-drab songbirds arriving under cover of darkness from Mexico to raise the next generation of vireos in a San Juan Island woods?

From a practical standpoint, Edward Howe Forbush put it well long ago when he wrote: "This vireo is one of the conservators of the forest—a caterpillar hunter of renown——one of a number of arboreal birds which guard the trees against the too destructive attacks of quickly multiplying scaly-winged hosts."

In other words, the vireo has its place and function in the web of life helping to keep biological balance in the forest. It also matters that this woodland remains relatively intact for migratory birds and butterflies and resident wildlife. By identifying the vireo's continuing use of this site, the value of preserving wild habitat is reinforced.

For me, there is more than the science and practicality of it. There is heart and soul, too. What does persevering to see a bird sing its heart out in the dappled green and gold canopy of a sublime woodland do for one's spirit? It makes mine soar. The vireos have their place in the world as we have ours. Sometimes those places overlap and we are privileged to observe the intimacies of their lives as we embrace our own. The experience may last only a moment and be gone. Upon reflection, that it matters to me is inconsequential. It is far more important that it matters to them.

~

The following spring: April 13. It was time for another breeding bird season. I drove to Lime Kiln to check on the old vireo nest. It was overcast and calm. The woods were awakening. The red alders were dropping their gold and scarlet catkins, the last ivory blooms of Indian plum were on the wane, and red columbine was still a promise. I found the vireo's braided cup intact in the madrone after months of hard rain and wind. The old tree had done its job well providing an abundance of fruit to hundreds of overwintering birds—robins and varied thrushes especially—that counted on its bounty.

I strolled down the trail and listened for the vireo's calls among the chatter of early spring birdsongs. When I played the audio tape to remind myself of the Cassin's phrasing, I got a reply, then another upslope. The vireos were home. I continued to explore and a few minutes later at the shoreline a vireo dropped down onto a cedar bough just above me. It launched into a series of short, loud, emphatic phrases that punctuated the air. The slight, olive-gray songbird was smaller than I remembered. His white spectacles illuminated those wonderful dark eyes that shone through the green dappled woods. I was thrilled to see him. I had hesitated to play the audio tape even once and felt guilty at having summoned *Vireo cassinii* on false pretenses. I moved on quickly leaving the suitor to prepare for the female's arrival. As one of the first breeding birds of spring to arrive, the Cassin's ebullient song owned the woods that day. It was a good feeling to know the little songbirds were back and that another vireo spring at Lime Kiln had begun.

4
ROCK GARDEN

For a short time in the spring, the tiny,
bright white flowers of tufted saxifrage
bloomed on chartreuse moss in cracks
and crevices of lime-infused bedrock
near Large Quarry at Lime Kiln. Other
succulent wildflowers contributed
to the unexpected floral bliss.

While waiting on the vireo nest, I returned to Lime Kiln to visit a cheerful wildflower niche. I had discovered the floral revelation years before, hiding in plain sight, while exploring the old quarries that dotted the hillside above the Whale Watch Park. My timing had to be perfect to see hundreds of bright yellow blooms emerging from the rock piles that remained from a colorful era in island history. Fingers crossed!

The story of industrializing the landscape we now call Lime Kiln began with European settlement dating back to the late 1850s. A chalky mineral called limestone, an important ingredient in the booming material growth of the West, was discovered on San Juan Island by Caleb Kennerly's Northwest Boundary Survey during the Pig War. The early economic fortunes of the island changed substantially with this development. The ensuing years of extensive lime production took a toll on island woodlands due to both the extraction process, especially along the shoreline, and the felling of timber to fuel the kilns. Work and riches came to islanders into the 1920s. The economy flourished, then fortunes changed. The Great Depression hit. Technology evolved and people moved on.

Fortunately, the U.S. Coast Guard acquired land for Lime Kiln Lighthouse, an important location for monitoring the navigation of cargo vessels through Haro Strait into Canada. In 1919, the new structure was opened. In 1984, Lime Kiln Point State Park was established and then Limekiln Preserve in 1997 thus securing over two hundred acres of shoreline and terrestrial habitats for conservation and recreation. Local historian Boyd Pratt's excellent book *"LIME, Quarrying and Limemaking in the San Juan Islands"* recounts the colorful tale of how the limemaking industry dramatically changed this landscape. Now, the woods continue to rebound from that industrial era. The natural healing is evident everywhere. Scars on the land and mining artifacts remain as a reminder of the past.

~

I had visited Lime Kiln briefly in April—before finding the Cassin's vireo nest—to catch the early bloom of the big-leaf maples that are an iconic presence there. It was an intense time of greening. The massive hardwoods, some two centuries old, were in full flower. Large cylindrical clusters of yellow-green blossoms hung several inches below celery and cinnabar leaf sheaths on the sturdy branches of *Acer macrophyllum*. The five-lobed leaves, up to a foot across, were just beginning to unfurl. When sunlight hit the trees, they radiated a stunning golden glow that infused every inch of the woods. The blooms were a bonanza for the bees and emerging butterflies. And, to me, it was the true awakening of absolute spring I had been waiting for.

Now, well into May, I promised myself an afternoon at Lime Kiln. I wanted to take my time sauntering and stopping along the way to reacquaint myself with the many forest dwellers that so often went unnoticed.

I began my walkabout at Westside Lake on a still, sunny afternoon with a soft blue sky overhead. As I stepped out of my car, I spotted a satyr anglewing butterfly fluttering about the cattails at the water's edge. It paused long enough for me to admire its crisp scalloped edges and bright orange, yellow and brown coloration announcing its recent emergence into the world. What a great way to start my afternoon.

I headed along the trail under a canopy of Douglas firs and red cedars. The sun sent splinters of bright light through breaks in the evergreens. The microhabitats of the Preserve bumped into one another, revealing a landscape of intriguing diversity and small wonders: wetlands hosted red-legged frogs and painted turtles; a grove of Sitka spruce lured brown creepers to build nests behind their fractured bark; herbaceous balds were rife with fragile ferns and mosses; and lichens dripped from the trees. Quaking aspens kept a discreet presence to the north.

There are thirteen abandoned quarries carved out of the bedrock into rough-edged coves flanked by a lush evergreen understory. In some places, tall grass meadows in front of these stone dugouts would soon be lush with splendid long-stemmed daisies and animated by blue dragonflies. As I passed by, Swainson's thrushes fluted their haunting songs, chipping sparrows asserted with rapid-fire trills, and pileated woodpeckers kept up their incessant drumbeats that resonated through the woods. The pileated seemed far superior to the woodworkers of long ago mining the forest with a master carpenter's skill. Snags were riddled with their rectangular-shaped cavities beckoning to smaller birds for nest sites when the pileated moved on.

Peering off trail, I could see the bones of old trees, fallen and decaying, and huge stumps with cross-cut saw scars among artifacts from both mining and logging operations that happened here long ago. These timbers now provided refuge for rough-skinned newts, northwest alligator lizards and Pacific sideband snails among others.

I detoured briefly to the meadow by the North Trail spur. As I scanned the margins of the open space, I caught a flash of bright color. Yes, a Julia's (formerly Sara's) orangetip butterfly fluttering just above the grass. It was a male, bright white above with orange wingtips edged in black. It was flying fast, a conspicuous display of vigor he hoped, I supposed, would attract a mate. What a great find! I had not seen the tiny Pieridae, kin to our endangered island marble butterfly, for several years and was thrilled by the encounter. It looked like it might be a good butterfly day.

Then, back on track through the woods. Interesting, as one becomes familiar with a place, the reference points along the trail take on seasonal importance. I passed an old Douglas fir snag where I had watched house wrens nesting predictably for several springs. Alas, the old-timer—badly decayed—had come down in a winter storm. The wrens had moved on. But, across the meadow, an olive-sided flycatcher had reclaimed its spring perch high atop another fir and was singing his "quick three beers" call right on cue. Then the buzzy, upturned notes of the black-throated gray warbler by the wetland. And always the boastful song of the Cassin's vireo blaring through the overstory. Ah, I knew its secret now: a beautiful woven nest of lichens and greens not far away where three young chicks were waiting to fledge under the protective gaze of the adult female.

The trail descended, transitioning from conifers to Pacific madrones and more big-leaf maples. This was the Quarry Trail also known as Coghlans' Trail. Preserve steward Doug McCutchen told me Cornelius and Catherine Coghlan were important figures in the fabric of life of the island between the 1880s and 1930s, particularly on the westside and San Juan Valley. Cornelius was the manager of the Limekiln operation for Henry Cowell. They lived just down the hill and Doug was pleased to see the trail honor them.

Then, into the open at the 200-foot elevation level. An imposing west-facing ridge several stories high loomed over the shoreline and the inland sea: Large Quarry. The hillside—founded on limestone-bearing sedimentary and volcanic rock—had been blasted away long ago and the remaining rubble and limestone tailings formed a talus slope that continued steeply down hill, back into the woods and on to the Whale Watch Park below. There was limestone rubble everywhere.

The cracks and crevices in the large rock face and piles of rock rubble adjacent to the talus slope portion of the trail (completed in 2016) were perfect receptacles for spring wildflowers. My timing was perfect. Here, succulent sedum and saxifrage were emerging from these limestone-etched nooks illuminating the vertical scape with a golden glow. I called this spot the Rock Garden. It was magnificent!

The main attraction was broad-leaved stonecrop (*Sedum spathulifolium*): small, fleshy bright yellow plants less than a foot tall. There were hundreds, if not thousands, of them cleaving to every crevice, crag and outcropping along the rugged slope and to the top of the

Broad-leaved Stonecrop.

rock wall. The plants were opportunist for sure having found a niche to thrive away from the hiker's boot. Their bright yellow, lance-shaped blooms, in flat-topped clusters, set upon crowds of fleshy rosettes of sage green, spoon-shaped leaves, radiated like five-pointed stars on the sunny west-facing slope. As a singular presence they might go unnoticed, but as an aggregate the stonecrop represented a stunning gathering of late spring cheer.

Sedum, from the Latin sedeo "to sit," referred to how stonecrop often settles on precarious ledges or precipices. Botanist Lewis J. Clark described the virtues of this beloved native from its cast-iron constitution and ability to creep up vertical rock faces to the beauty of "… a low spreading canopy of brightest golden flowers that continue a long period to gladden the grey rocks."

I continued down the talus slope to get a better look at the flora, surrounded at every turn by the stars—or so it seemed. Nestled low and unassuming in crevices between the rubble and stonecrop was the delicate small-flowered alumroot. It was the first of two saxifrages I knew at the site. Again, quoting Clark: "a favored perch of *H. micrantha* is a creviced cliff face, often shaded and sometimes looking down on sea or lake. Here it is charming with its mist of tiny white blooms dancing on slender arched stems above a cluster of handsome leaves."

Working my way along the talus rubble, limestone shards crunching under my boot, I spotted another beautiful wildflower with a shy presence. The blooms were white, five-petaled and quite small growing on slender threads out of a bed of yellow and chartreuse moss. It was tufted saxifrage (*Saxifraga cespitosa)*. When I first encountered it several years before, it was a mystery to me. I took photos and emailed them to Land Bank botanist Eliza Habegger for a consult. She identified my puzzlement as (likely) tufted saxifrage. Saxifrages are hardy, good-natured plants; their name means rock breaker, for they grow in such tiny crevices that one might think they are breaking through the stone. The environs of Large Quarry were a perfect habitat for the elegant, pristine blooms. Every stone nook padded with moss seemed to house a little fist of the sublime flowers.

As I clambered about the rockery, being careful not to slip on the steep slope, I wondered what wildlife might be using this lush, if rugged, terrain. The throngs of lemon-yellow stonecrop were sitting high on stout, fleshy stems as if to say to the pollinators: "Right this way. Here we are!" Ah, there was a tiny echo azure butterfly nectaring on the blooms. Yellow-faced bumble bees in perfect color-coded harmony brushed the petals. The first blue dragonflies of the season darted about. A handsome garter snake rested in the grass. I had been told there were sharp-tailed snakes, too, but luck wasn't with me that day. I bent down to get a closer look at the rockery and spied a tiny abandoned shell shaped like a nautilus. Could it be the Pacific sideband snail?

This wildflower spectacle would be short-lived. The alumroot and saxifrage—the first plants to appear in this stonecrop succession—were already beginning to fade, so I sat a spell on a flat-topped stone along the talus slope to take in the extravagant scene. I looked up into the cracks and crevices of the immense bedrock wall and wondered what birds might be nesting in the precarious yet protected niches. And, who sang the stonecrop into bloom? Maybe my old friend Vireo from up the way. When did stonecrop first beckon the bees, I wanted to know? I was sorry to have missed that moment. I continued my musing and soon violet-green swallows swooped by with their exuberant air. And, always, the cawing of crows nearby.

What an extraordinary niche: wild, rugged, wind-blown, rain-soaked most of the year, but for a few short weeks in the spring, a sanctuary of scintillating wildflowers to take one's breath away. They had to be hardy plants to survive these stony reaches, but the blooms of alumroot and saxifrage possessed a delicate air of fragility that almost made the quarry blush.

Come to think of it, the entire island was truly a rock garden. How many times had I driven past a rock wall chock full of sedum and barely noticed? But this place was special. Not hidden but largely going unnoticed. I waited all year for these precious days - hoping my timing would be right. This year, I was in luck. The stars were out. That evening I wrote in my journal: "To find such joy in a little yellow, five-pointed star … Thrilling!"

Yes, I was aware of the ephemeral nature of the wildflower bloom, but also of another time constraint with a more permanent impact. Young conifers—Douglas firs, red cedars, and sapling madrones—had taken hold along the slope and were growing fast. Several years ago, this space was wide open and brightly lit by the sun. Now, these young trees were casting shade upon the scene. This was a wild-flower habitat already in transition. Stonecrop needed light and moisture. It would not be long before the conifers reclaimed this patch of bedrock and the wildflowers would struggle to bloom in the shade. What a good lesson on the ever-changing nature of our world. And all the more reason to sit still a few minutes more with these beautiful flowers.

~

Before I headed back up the trail to Westside Lake, I stood at the Vista Point and took in the view of Haro Strait and Vancouver Island beyond. A red warning sign cautioned about getting too close to the edge as the hillside remained fragile and unstable from mining operations long ago. I happily obliged and stepped back. Only days before, a friend mentioned having stood at this very spot and watched Dall's porpoises foraging just offshore in Haro Strait.

Stories abound about these woods and hillsides having been clear cut for the kilns. In talking with Lime Kiln Point State Park Ranger David Halpern, the details remained unclear. Old photographs show the kilns, warehouses, a boarding house and other crudely crafted structures that dominated the shoreline and west slopes of San Juan Island during that period. Remnants of some of those buildings remain today. Aerial photos from the 1930s showed open savannah along these shores; sheep were grazed there. That still rang true. Gazing to the far slopes, I was surprised to see many open, rocky balds. It wasn't densely forested at all. Ranger Halpern reported that today, much of the woodlands in the vicinity of Lime Kiln were forested with conifers between sixty and eighty years ago.

Discussions continue regarding how much of the forest near Lime Kiln was felled for the kilns. Historians know that local farmers and other land owners cleared their properties throughout the island at substantial profit hauling hardwood to the kilns by wagon. Cutting conifers to fuel the kilns on San Juan, Orcas and smaller islands took a toll on old growth forests. But just how much of Lime Kiln was actually forested in those times remains unclear.

~

I returned up the hill toward the backside of Large Quarry. The ground was littered with woody debris from a late spring wind. Just off the trail to the north was a magnificent old big-leaf maple. It was likely well over one hundred years old with deeply furrowed gray bark, mosses, lichens and licorice ferns. A bit broken but still a nursery for new life. As expected, there were dozens of yellow-faced bumble bees in the wilting blooms and an orange-crowned warbler picking insects off the dinner-plate-sized leaves. And there, a mourning cloak butterfly nectaring on the last of the blooms—keeping its fluttering self always in the energizing sun.

Imagine the stories that fine old tree could recall about the First People of this land, and what these trees meant to them long ago—and to this day. At least one tribe called the maple the Paddle Tree for the wood's use in propelling their canoes. Wood, bark and fiber were also used for spindle whorls, combs, lures, toys, masks, clothing and twine among many other utilities. The sap was used as syrup. As I turned away from the beautiful, broad-leaved masterpiece of the forest, a black-headed grosbeak's rambling chortle sang me along the trail.

Before I left, I explored the eastside of Large Quarry. More rock piles edged the site. The sleeping stones were covered by dense layers of lichens and chartreuse moss. The ground was uneven, strewn with fragments of limestone as if workers long ago left in a hurry and did not clean up. I picked up a shard. The small light gray stone had a granular texture that revealed slender white etchings of lime. Limestone is a form of calcite or calcium carbonate. In the San Juans this mineral dates from the last phase of the Paleozoic Era and its appearance here was the result of convoluted occurrences of geologic and biological processes and plate tectonic convergence I will leave to the geologists to ponder and explain.

This part of the quarry seemed relatively undisturbed. Young madrones and saplings of fir and cedar nudged each other in this natural nursery. Great (flannel) mullein was emerging from the rocky substrate. By June, its large spikes with soft, hairy, lance-shaped leaves would bring another inflorescence of bright yellow blooms to this scape. A Bewick's wren buzzed from atop one of the rock piles occasionally adding short, loud whistles to its call.

As I moved through the gathering of young trees, I startled a ragged fox: grizzled gray on her muzzle and back, a white tip on the tail and coal-black ears and legs. She was standing near the huge stone wall in the shadow of a young madrone. Her dark, deep-set eyes expressed caution—hers and mine—and I retreated to the refrain of cawing crows watching from a nearby Douglas fir snag. It wasn't the first time I had seen that fine old fox and likely would not be the last. This was her domain far more than mine.

I kept exploring and turned toward a gathering of young redcedars. "Well, hello there," I said to a fine Pacific tree frog sunning itself on a cedar bough. "I almost missed you." Frogs are usually shy souls. Not this one. Its glistening lime green skin perfectly matched the tips of the bough. I moved closer and could see heart beats beneath its shining skin. It watched me but did not move. I did not go closer. It was a perfect moment. All seemed right in both of our worlds. I continued on, offering my gratitude to the frog who appeared to be continuing its midday meditation.

Around a bend in the stone wall, past newly blooming thimbleberry, a hidden fox trail wound down the slope in front of Large Quarry. Every crevice was crammed with fresh stonecrop—a constellation of yellow stars in the rockery. The images took my breath away. The going got steep, though, and I backed out onto level ground.

As I turned into the open, an easy breeze kicked up two western tiger swallowtails who fluttered ahead of me. Again, I sat a spell. The depth of diversity in these woods was humbling. I would have liked nothing better than to spend the rest of spring observing the ebb and flow of wildlife here. Certainly, the forest was filled with bird songs—soon to be quiet, though, as nesting continued and silence was a good protection against predators. And I was eager to find Moss' elfin, a tiny brown and gold butterfly whose host plant was the dazzling stonecrop. It might spend its entire life in a small patch of this quarry, the pupae for the next generation overwintering here for a next spring emergence. Brown elfins were there, too, likely keying on the madrones.

I wondered who was caretaking this magnificent landscape—perhaps the audacious crows or that watchful fox? Or was it the wind that came surging in from the North Pacific occasionally dismantling the tops of these old trees and staking its claim to a rugged, wonderful realm?

It was nearly time to go. It had been an afternoon filled with butterflies and golden wildflowers. I still had one more stop to make on the way back to Westside Lake.

5

MONA'S WORLD

A Pacific sideband snail munched on lichens in the westside woods, her mahogany and gold-swirled shell perfectly camouflaged in the duff where she might live for fifteen years.

W here's Mona? I had been asking that question since I began my spring strolls at Lime Kiln looking for Cassin's vireo. I was eager to find my old friend of the forest—that enigmatic, little mollusk that so often goes undetected in the woods: *Monadenia fidelis*, the Pacific sideband snail.

"A snail?" you ask. And I reply, "Yes. She is intriguing and beautiful!" My life as an island naturalist has, over time, veered from investigating the bold and dramatic species in our midst toward the small and quiet creatures that hold the webs of life together. The unassuming beckon me.

I first met Mona in the early spring of 2010. I was walking a woodland trail at The Labs and, as I stopped to clamber over an old Douglas fir that had come down in a storm, there she was clinging to a cedar bough in the shadow of the broken tree. I had been looking for sideband snails casually on my walks but never taken the quest seriously. This snail was hiding in plain sight. She was beautiful, with light and dark-golden whorls on her mahogany shell. There was just a hint of her raspberry-hued body peaking out of the spiral. I took her photo, then marked the length of her carapace with a piece of paper. Later, at home, it measured one and one-eighth inches.

I stayed with her a spell. She seemed vulnerable in the open, so I gently moved her, still on her bough, just a few inches out of harm's way. She retreated into her shell.

I was thrilled to have found Mona. Now that I had her image in my mind, I suspected it was not the last I would see of this tiny, engaging terrestrial gastropod.

~

Walking back toward Westside Lake from my wildflower walk at Large Quarry, I knew where to look for the sideband snail. The primary requirements for Mona's presence seemed to be moisture, woody debris and often rocky substrates with a gathering of mosses and lichens for shelter. A small, seasonal wetland just up from the talus slope usually held the prize. The jumble of alders, firs, spruce and willows was moist from spring rain—just her style—but after several minutes of searching the duff, there was no sign of Mona.

I retreated toward the lake checking the understory as I went. I stopped at a luminous patch of moss beside a pile of rock rubble. Eyes on the forest floor. No luck. Then, as I rose, I noticed ocean spray was beginning to flower overhead. I admired its latticework of buds, soon to be cascading pyramids of creamy-white blooms, but what was that dark spot about ten feet high in the foliage? I took out my binoculars for a look. It was Mona with her little reddish nose in a clump of light grayish/green lichen on a burnished brown stem. "Well, there you are!" I said. It was the first time I had seen the land snail off the forest floor. I thought Mona stayed grounded on terra firma. Ha! I had a lot to learn about terrestrial mollusks. The late afternoon light was fading fast but there was time to admire her chestnut shell and count six black and gold whorls. Her carapace was deeply etched with scratches and scars—perhaps a testimony of many years living in this woods. I took a snapshot and inadvertently brushed her branch; she recoiled into her calciferous shell. "Oh, sorry, Mona," I offered. Yes, it was time to move on, but not before a quick scan of the mossy rock rubble—her domain. It was full-on spring; the breeding season. I suspected there were more sideband snails nearby.

Pacific sidebands are the largest native land snail in the Northwest—a common species of gastropod ranging over a variety of habitats but partial to moist, mixed forest ecosystems. On San Juan, they are often found in the duff and under logs feeding on mosses, lichens and some herbaceous plants.

Sidebands are small and slow growing, maturing at under two inches in eight to ten years. These snails are hermaphrodites (both male and female reproductive organs) and perhaps best known in popular literature for throwing "love darts" at one another during their elaborate courtships. The javelin-like darts, made of cartilage or calcium carbonate, contain hormones that may enhance reproductive success. The trait seems to add to Mona's mystique.

My fascination with *Monadenia* was simple. It was always fun to encounter her in the woods. She is cryptic most of the year, often seen in the spring. A true Northwest native, the variation in the color of the beautiful land snail's spiral shell engaged me. From this snail's deep chestnut to swirls of black and gold, I wondered at Nature's mechanism of camouflage in this wooded world. Mona's disappearing acts were many, sometimes right before my eyes so perfect was her form among the leaves and litter of the forest.

As well, Mona climbs trees to twenty feet, always moves forward with her large, flat foot, often takes long naps in dry summers (aestivation) to preserve moisture, may sleep away the winter tucked in a cradle of mosses and lichens along a talus slope like Large Quarry, and will live perhaps fifteen years in this realm. She is a distant cousin to clams, oysters, squid and octopus.

Mona's jobs in the woods are specific. She is a recycler: digesting leaves, litter, fungi and such from the understory and releasing the nutrients that support other creatures. And, sadly, she is prey for many forest dwellers including birds, frogs, beetles and raccoons. But I don't despair, having watched her slow-motion life among the sword ferns and Sitka spruce. She appears to be a survivor under that sturdy sculptured shell. History tells us that land snails have been on earth for at least 150 million years. Her survival strategy seems to be working.

I was pleased to have found the beautiful sideband snail—especially witnessing her tree-climbing capability. As dusk approached, I wondered if Mona—a nocturnal species—would continue her climb up the ocean spray in search of more tasty lichens. A lofty goal and I suspected she was in no hurry.

I retired that night thinking fondly of Mona out and about the forest making her living. She might sleep under a canopy of red cedars and stars, snug in the spray or leaf litter, and lulled by the sounds of the woodland: the Swainson's thrushes' soulful song, the hooting of a great horned owl, and light spring rain falling softly on her magnificent shell.

6

NIGHT LIFE

*During late May and June,
the rare sand-verbena moth rested
on yellow sand-verbena. The "owlet"
was leading its brief adult life as
an influential nighttime pollinator
near the dunes at Cattle Point.*

There I was, on hands and knees, combing through patches of low-slung, sand-loving succulent plants—in the dark—looking for a cryptic owlet moth that lived a mostly subterranean existence on the dunes at American Camp. The prize was the sand-verbena moth and these plants were the key to its tenuous existence on the island, and on the planet. I used my newly purchased headlamp to light the way through a dimly moonlit world that held intriguing clues to the presence of this beautiful, elusive and rare insect.

I had wondered about the secretive moth for years and worked literally on top of its home surveying rare island marble butterflies. While intrigued by the moth's presence, time always seemed to slip away from me during the busy field season.

Butterflies, like island marble, get most of the attention. They are beautiful, ethereal, and flutter across sun-drenched landscapes as symbols of Nature's perfection. Moths. Well, they come out at night, are often drab in coloration, fly with frenzy around bright lights, and don't have the awe-inspiring survival stories of their cousins. Ah, but they do!

The sand-verbena moth likely has been struggling for survival on the dunes at American Camp for decades—hiding in plain sight, if in the dark. They play vitally important roles as night-time pollinators—especially in an age when bee and butterfly populations are plummeting. These moths are doing remarkable work to help keep the webs of life intact and functioning in a world where biodiversity is at risk in dwindling and degraded habitats.

Now, finally, it was time to explore the world of these enigmatic, fuzzy-headed souls.

~

The sand-verbena moth is a Northwest native. It is nocturnal, tiny, with a wingspan of less than two inches, and cryptically colored in shades of buff and brown; conspicuous light yellow and black lines on the forewings make it nearly invisible on the dunes. It spends a good portion of its time below ground during immature stages of its life. The moth got its name from its association with the native beach-loving plant yellow sand-verbena (*Abronia latifolia*). The verbena, its only host plant, inhabits dunes, beaches, spits, and shrubs in a narrow, specialized coastal zone in the rainshadow world of the San Juan Archipelago. The cheerful, bright yellow succulent, while highly visible in large aggregates, grows close to the sand and is an unassuming presence. Thus, both the moth and its host plant live generally unnoticed lives at the south end of the island.

The cryptic moth had been studied in the Gulf Islands of British Columbia since 1995 where it is listed as endangered. Field investigations began in the San Juans in the early 2000s, but its presence on the dunes had been overshadowed by the more visible and charismatic island marble butterfly. It is known in coastal sand dunes in Island, Clallam and San Juan Counties in Washington State and in the Strait of Georgia region of British Columbia.

~

My acquaintance with this tiny owlet moth began with a brief encounter some time before my hands and knees sojourn into their dark world at the dunes. In late April 2017, while monitoring island marbles and western tailed blue butterflies on the backbeach at American Camp, I ran into endangered species biologist Karen Reagan who was on site doing reconnaissance for a sand-verbena moth survey that would commence in late May. She came down from the dunes excited to report she had located a sand-verbena moth larva burrowed in the sand. Karen asked if I would like to see one of the tiny insects. Of course!

We walked back up the sandy ridge along the edge of the dunes into its habitat. The stalks of spent sand-verbena were poking their cinnamon selves out of the glacially-tilled dunes looking like pudgy, oversized cigars. This year's crop of plants would soon be flowering, producing tiny, five-lobed blooms perched in rounded heads on short, stout stalks. The larval stage of the moth (having dwelled in the sand all winter) was emerging now at night to feed on the succulent host plant's waxy green leaves. While the adult moths are night-flyers, the larvae (caterpillars) can be found during daylight hours.

Karen knew where she was going. She scanned the dunes. "There could be one there or there," she announced, pointing out a small gathering of plants as we strode across the sand. Then abruptly, she dropped to her knees and started digging.

After a few scoops of sand, the biologist sighed: "Oh, oh. Nothing there. They do move around, though. See those little tracks in the sand?" she motioned toward tiny, squiggly indentations in the substrate.

Karen kept looking and digging more holes each four or five inches deep. "Ah ha!" she exclaimed. "Here's one!" and she proudly lifted from the substrate a late-instar larva that looked like a fleshy, segmented, light-gray worm. She cupped it in the palm on her hand clearly pleased with the prize. It was intriguing to see this little, translucent cutworm curled up in her grasp. I took photographs, then Karen laid the larva gently back in its hole in the sand. We watched as it excavated its way underground again. Fascinating! A true subterranean.

Karen continued her moth tutorial. The key to finding the larvae was to look for herbivory on the crescent-shaped leaves of the sand-verbena. She bent down to show me. I saw the moth's signature scalloped chew marks on many plants.

I was delighted with our discoveries. As we walked back toward the parking lot Karen joked: "This is why it is cool to hang out with biologists." She was right. Our time together was a great introduction to the SVM.

~

Time got away from me, as it often did, but having seen the moth larva my fascination with the SVM endured. I made two outings to the dunes in May, awaiting the adult moth's emergence, but the weather turned fickle and intermittent rain squalls dampened my expectations.

On June 8, I joined DNR zoologist John Fleckenstein and pollinator specialist Julie Combs near South Beach as they began their formal presence/absence surveys of the moth as part of a major assessment of the species for possible endangered species designation. Nearly twenty years before, John had rediscovered the island marble butterfly at American Camp after its supposed extinction on Vancouver Island in 1908. He had already done significant field work with COFU (shorthand for *COpablepharon FUscum*) and was eager for field time with the moth before his upcoming retirement. Dr. Combs had a long history studying pollinator/host plant relationships and was tasked that season with mapping *Abronia's* abundance within COFU's known range.

John set up a blacklight trap in a stand of sand-verbena by a willow thicket along the backbeach. The small, lightweight device was designed to lure the moths to its ultraviolet light and hold them harmlessly for identification and release. It rained. It stopped. It rained again. We waited and were rewarded, near twilight, with the appearance of several moth species including one likely sand-verbena moth in the trap. But the weather was dreadful and conditions poor for making positive identifications. It would not stop raining for a long time.

I was happy to have gotten that first fleeting glimpse of a sand-verbena moth. I would learn later that "look-alikes" were present and that, on the first night of trapping, great care was being taken to ensure all identifications were scrupulously correct. As I left, John and Julie were headed—undaunted—to the dunes to set up two more traps. We hoped to get together later as conditions improved.

~

In the days that followed, I persevered on my own. My wandering was far flung on the dunes sometimes working my way toward Mt. Finlayson and Cattle Point across subtle terraces of sand along the west-facing slopes. These benches are the erosive products of a series of receding sea levels left behind after the melt of the last glacial flow of the Pleistocene Epoch here.

In the post-glacial era, the tilled landscape had slowly vegetated. Wind, wild birds, and mammals promoted seed dispersal. The First People were active thousands of years before tending and utilizing natural resources. The Coast Salish were great land stewards then, and brilliant teachers today, sharing their wisdom in partnership with park managers. With European settlement beginning in the mid-1840s, changes to the dune habitat were accelerated, especially by formal agricultural pursuits.

The dunes face Haro Strait, shifting and continuing to erode at the whim of strong Pacific storms. Deep-rooted plants like the yellow sand-verbena help stabilize the habitat. The vegetation and contour of the dunes change dramatically. The webs of life in this

Island Marble Butterfly.

rugged but fragile world have been transforming and evolving, too.

My movements on the dunes were carefully choreographed to ensure doing no harm to the moth or to the island marbles that I knew were also nearby. I walked along fox and deer trails, a moonscape of rabbit warrens, on open expanses of sand without vegetation, and established transects for surveying the butterflies (with permission from the park). This was fragile territory. Going off trail meant the possibility of trampling host plants or unwittingly disturbing those moth larvae that were underground.

The yellow sand-verbena was profuse, spreading across the landscape in dense mats of plump, succulent leaves as far as the eye could see. Its thick, fleshy, hairy stems hugged the ground. Those tiny, bright lemony blooms are tubular—without petals—arranged in umbels like shiny, waxy bouquets in the sand. The leaves give off a sticky secretion that attracts the sand and adds to the bulk of the plant. This added weight helps anchor the little sand-verbena in the wind. Such a marvel of plant architecture! The huge gathering of plants provided perfect conditions for the moths.

I found signs of the moth's presence everywhere among the verbena. I spied many circular chunks munched out of *Abronia* leaves by the moth larvae, much like Karen had shown me in April. Those chew marks were a giveaway that the moth larvae were active at night.

I saw tiny tracks on the substrate, too. Were they the meanderings of moth larvae or something else? And there was strange digging in the sand: red foxes or rabbits? Both were familiar residents in the dunes.

The richness of the terrain was breathtaking. There were gullies and washes carved out by Pacific winds flush with colorful native flora including seashore lupine, bi-color lupine, vetch and harvest brodiaea. The beach morning glory was particularly enticing. Its white, funnel-shaped flowers were heavily washed with lavender and stretched in large, viny patches across the sand. Here was another low-slung plant with deep tap roots that partnered with yellow sand-verbena in stabilizing the substrate. Dune grasses proliferated. Bracken ferns were everywhere. When checking the unfolding blooms of tumble mustard, I sometimes found tiny, orange eggs or the miniscule larvae of the island marble butterflies that hatched among those yellow flowers.

Down the way, newly arrived American goldfinch were foraging on seaside fiddleneck. The bees buzzed. I found a little native bee having taken up residence in a hollowed-out sand-verbena root. Beautiful! Breeding birds, especially savannah sparrows, flitted across the plain. The sparrows, as ground nesters, had tiny, woven nests of grass tucked in the folds of the prairie across Pickett's Lane. Common butterflies, including painted ladies, Milbert's tortoiseshell and red admirals, were a constant presence. Cabbage white butterflies—the common island marble look-alike—were there, too. The scene was set for the adult sand-verbena moths to emerge and claim their place on and above the dunes. It was only a matter of time and opportunity.

~

A week after my time with John and Julie, conditions were ideal: calm, clear and 60 degrees. I arrived at American Camp well before twilight. I planned my search at a spot I called Fiddleneck Forest for the massive blooms of the wildflower seaside fiddleneck that formed the perfect edge for acres of blooming sand-verbena. Waiting for twilight and the moths, I watched a male island marble hill-topping along the ridge just above the fiddleneck, and listened to the familiar *wichity-wichity* call of a common yellowthroat in a thicket nearby. I stood enjoying the butterfly as the light sparkled off Haro Strait. Then, I sauntered along the backbeach admiring the prickly big-headed sedge, the fiery scarlet hues of sheep sorrel, and checking dozens of verbena flower heads looking for signs of the moth. The verbena was even growing in the crevices of driftwood. I found leaves that were blistered and had been nibbled upon. Yes, this was a good spot.

The marble retreated. The light faded fast. It was the in-between time when the silence was broken only by the gentle pulse of incoming tide meeting South Beach. At nine-thirty, as I watched the transition to night, a white-crowned sparrow began to call. Its highly recognizable vocal, a two-toned whistle followed by a series of jumbled notes ending with a buzzy trill, resonated across the shore: "Oh, me, pretty, pretty me!" it pronounced. The sparrow's call rang out three times as the light disappeared in the western sky. Then, the calling stopped and, simultaneously, two moths emerged twenty feet east of my station in the sand and fluttered low over the verbena. Yes, there was COFU. I moved closer. The moths quickly keyed on the umbels of sand-verbena, perching on the stems, almost covering the sturdy yellow flower heads and unfurling their long, slender reddish-brown proboscises (tongues) to dip into the trumpet-shaped blooms and uptake nectar. They supped meticulously from tepal to tepal then, with a quick flutter, were on to the next plant. The moths' host plants dominated the scape, like hundreds of yellow points of light in the sand illuminated by my lantern.

COFU were surprisingly easy to spot with their buffy, earth-toned bodies and forewings, clearly displaying the yellow and black lines that were diagnostic of the species. And those fuzzy heads! Rich, golden hairs adorned the brows of the little moths and tightly swept back a bit like shaggy crewcuts. I checked my watch. It was just ten o'clock.

I put on my headlamp. The moths were attracted to its beam and did not shy away. I was delighted to be getting my long-awaited close encounter with these rare noctuids. Such beautiful animals. When my light hit them just right, I noted a silver sheen on their scaly wings—an almost iridescent shine. "Ah, silver moon dust on their wings," I thought to myself.

COFU flew methodically from one plant to the next, adept at climbing about the blooms doing their jobs as master pollinators. The short hops were effortless—almost buoyant—in their execution. Hungry, I suspected. They were just beginning their nighttime forays that would likely conclude before the turn to morning. With each stopover, the moths were sating their appetites and also transferring the precious pollen from plant to plant.

I took photographs. At one point, a moth fluttered over and landed on my hand just for a moment, and then was gone. Attracted to my light, I surmised. I settled in the sand, surrounded by beach grass, verbena and lupine, put my camera down, and absorbed the serenity with these rare moths fluttering about the wildflowers in the dark. There were other moths, too, keying on the verbena and landing on their leaves. Their identification would have to wait.

I watched for about forty minutes. I found I could keep track of the moths by their copper eyeshine glistening in my light. COFU had a graceful nature. The moths dipped down into their host plants with tiny, delicate feet. Testing the blooms. Where to stay and where to go, both nectaring and simultaneously acting as go-betweens in collecting and transferring pollen with each visitation. They rested on sand-encrusted leaves, sometimes stopping momentarily on the sand in their camouflaged capes and disappearing as if an illusion. When a subtle gust of wind appeared, I watched one tiny moth relinquish the power of its wings and relax into the breeze floating a short way before executing a soft landing on a piece of beach grass.

It was dark now, although the waning gibbous moon provided a glow that tempered pitch black. I decided it was best to head for the car. Walking past a makeshift driftwood sculpture I spotted another moth, and then another. There was eyeshine all about. I recalled that less than a week before, I had seen a fox kit digging in the sand nearby. I wondered if it had been excavating for moth larvae much as Karen had shown me months before. While it was tempting to stay, I reluctantly kept going. A killdeer's piercing, high call rang through the dark bidding me good-bye.

At home, I downloaded to my computer the images of the first two moths I found. There were the furry heads, those light and dark strips along the forewings, and the tiny bronze eyes. One of the moths looked fresh, as though it had just emerged from the chrysalis. The other had a severely torn wing. Was it old or had it encountered a predator, I wondered? The tears and scars on butterfly and moth wings tell part of the history of their short lives. The images clearly showed how camouflaged the moths were against the beach grass and sand. Nearly invisible, I suspected, to night predators including bats and tiger beetles.

Later, some of the other moths were identified as Edward's beach moth, lesser Wainscot moth, and Isabella tiger moth. It was nice to know that COFU was not the only nocturnal pollinator at work along the back shore. The moths were a wonder of form and function. Watching them living their lives in this dark world was like uncovering a secret.

~

I was enchanted by the moth and eager for more encounters. Two weeks later, I joined John, Julie and contract biologist Claire Crawbuck along the bluff trail at Cattle Point. It was nearing the end of the flight season (the adult sand-verbena moth lives less than three weeks, at best) but there was still work to be done.

We arrived forty minutes to twilight. The weather was greatly improved: calm at 55 degrees. John set up four light traps, from north to south, alternately among beach grass, sand-verbena and bare sandy substrate. The sun disappeared as he finished the setup. We waited only a few minutes before the shiny sliver of the moon threw a silver sheen on Haro Strait from a clear, crisp sky. It was "moth time" once more, as Julie liked to say.

They had no luck at the first light trap embedded in beach grass, and only "fuzzy imposters" with red eyeshine appeared at trap #2. But the action picked up. There were more imposters in trap #3. We were all down on hands and knees inspecting the vegetation around the trap. Young Claire—a university graduate student in biology still pondering the subject for her master's thesis—seemed especially adept at catching the night flyers. Soon, she scrambled our way over the sand presenting a single sand-verbena moth poised on a calyx (the trumpet-shaped bracts about the stamens on the yellow sand-verbena). Claire had a good eye and a knack for capturing— if only momentarily—the moths. Her enthusiasm brightened the dark. No moths in the trap, though, and it was on to #4.

The final trap was positioned in a blowout of bare sand close to the edge of the bluff. There was a clear line of sight for the moths from the nearby blooming sand-verbena and the light in the trap. Bingo!

The air was full of the flutterings of the little night owlets. They were in and out of the trap, alighting on our clothes, and headed back and forth to their host plants to nectar. They were easy to catch. John and Julie used nets, and Claire continued using her hands. Getting these momentary close looks at the moths was thrilling. Even more so, was letting them go.

The team sorted effectively through the moths in the trap. "That's it!" John exclaimed. Or: "No, too small; too gray; wrong body type; doesn't have a fuzzy head; red eyeshine; the shape is all wrong." Weeks of working with the noctuids had made identification easy now. The work was done in under an hour. The final tally was three SVMs in trap #4 and at least seven others in the vicinity. I heard John say, "Fabulous!" quietly under his breath. A kind and gentle man who clearly loved his work, it was heartening to watch how carefully John handled the tiny insects and the clear admiration he seemed to have for the fragile flyers. I knew this rare creature was in respectful and capable hands.

We sauntered back to the car to check our notes for the evening. Every outing for these biologists brought new revelations. The lesson that night had been observing that the moth activity was almost exclusively on the bare sand and nearby sand-verbena—not in the beach-grassy understory. There was plenty of open space around that fourth light trap. Nectar sources abounded and the moths had a clear view of one another which enhanced their opportunities for mating. It had been a good night. I bid adieu to John, Julie and Claire not likely to encounter them again before season's end. It had been thrilling to see so many moths in the warm, dark air at Cattle Point and spend time with these dedicated folks.

∼

I saw the moths again before their flight season ended but only in a brief encounter while working on another project. It had been a very good season for the little owlet moths; the yellow sand-verbena bloom had been the best in many years. COFU were thriving. Before this spring, I had paid little mind to the moth or to nighttime pollinators in general. My time with these largely unseen, understated and often unappreciated insects had been enlightening. They were playing a vitally important role in the functioning of the dune ecosystem at American Camp by literally transforming the landscape through pollination and helping boost ecological health. COFU was a great support to the daytime work of the butterflies, birds and bees. It is intriguing to wonder how the sand-verbena moth and the yellow sand-verbena might have adapted to one another over the ages to produce this current perfectly conceived and highly successful partnership. And seeing island marble along the way had been a reminder that they were charting their own endangered species course on the dunes, too. Yes, it was all connected and part of this secret world of the sand-verbena moth.

7

AMERICAN AVOCET & THE LONG-AGO LAGOON

At the turn into summer, an off course American avocet took refuge at Old Town Lagoon while seeking its way home.

An American avocet stood on one blue leg in brine-filled Old Town Lagoon. It was unmistakable: a large, long-necked shorebird about eighteen inches tall standing perfectly still, ankle deep, in the salty green muck. The dapper bird's head, neck and breast shone cinnamon with a pinkish glow—the color of a late spring sunrise. Its belly and backside glistened white. Sooty black wings were folded over its back revealing snowy patches that would register as a V-line in flight. Its other steely stilt was tucked to its belly. The defining detail, a long, slender, black bill—dramatically upturned—appeared polished by the light into a midnight sheen. What a magnificent bird!

It was noon when I stopped upslope from the lagoon at the Jakle's parking lot. I had spent the morning birding the south end of the island and was making one last scan of the shoreline before heading home. I was surprised to see the avocet. It was a rare species for the archipelago, having been recorded only twice in the 1980s across San Juan Channel on Lopez. Avocets breed in eastern Washington, among other places. What was it doing here—in June—on the wrong side of the North Cascade Range?

I stood for several minutes watching the avocet through my binoculars. I hailed a fellow birder to confirm the sighting, then headed to the beach for a closer look.

~

It was 60 degrees; four days shy of the summer solstice. A five-knot breeze escorted clouds of insignificance across a canvas of pale blue. It was a perfect afternoon to observe this beautiful bird.

Old Town is a triangular-shaped saltwater lagoon. Unlike its siblings, Jakle's Lagoon and Third Lagoon to the southeast that are nestled against a forest of mature Douglas firs, western red cedars, and western hemlock, this tiny, shallow respite of brackish water transitions into grassland—once prairie—that historically extended over the ridge to Haro Strait.

The lagoon is strongly influenced by precipitation, evaporation, and wind that result in fluctuations in water temperature and salinity. Storm surges sometimes inundate the lagoon in the winter. Old Town often goes dry in the summer.

I walked slowly along the cobbled shore of Fourth of July Beach toward the lagoon and the avocet, following the line of wrack where tangles of glistening seagrass, porcelain clam shells, miniscule crabs with orange pinchers, torn bird feathers and briny debris defined the last high tide. I clambered over driftwood, bleached gray by tidal assault and sun, looking for a spot to sit. A fox trail led me to a patch that would do. It had matted turf among the sprawling vines of silver bursage (*Ambrosia chamissonis*).

The avocet watched me arrive but only slightly shifted its stance at its feeding station at the north end of the lagoon. Four herringbone striped gadwalls dabbled at the opposite end of the shallows. A flock of violet-green swallows swooped low over the water devouring clutches of swirling insects. Two rambunctious killdeer scurried and ranted along the drift.

The American avocet is one of North America's most striking shorebirds. Long ago, ornithologists often referred to its showy presence. The sight of its graceful form lingered long in their memories and in their journals.

The "blue shank" or "blue stocking," as the avocet was called by hunters, was an intense forager, first sweeping its long, flat, upturned bill across the muck and snatching aquatic insects and tiny crabs from the substrate, then probing the brine methodically for subterranean worms. Avocets are usually group feeders. And noisy. I never heard this bird make a sound that might betray its solitary presence.

As time passed, the avocet continued its stroll and scurry about the flats and along the edges of the lagoon. It seemed to bob its head in satisfaction of a good catch, but more likely was only swallowing hard. Occasionally, it stopped to shake water off its plumage and to preen with its needle-like bill. There was eloquent intention to every stroke of that fine tool. After all, the name avocet comes from the Italian "avosetta" which translates to "graceful bird."

At two-thirty, the avocet stopped feeding, turned its head, tucked its shapely bill beneath the feathers on its back, and went to sleep. I used the break to take notes and reflect on the historic site.

~

Wolves roamed this land until the early 1850s when Indigenous people—the Northern Straits/Coast Salish—were still the prominent human presence on the island. In 1851, the Hudson's Bay Company set up a salmon salting station on Griffin Bay to gain a presence on the island, and in 1853 established Belle Vue Sheep Farm just over the ridge from the lagoon. With the coming of the HBC and the success of their sheep stations and agricultural activities, word of the many values of San Juan spread rapidly. British, American and European settlers rushed in for a land grab displacing the First People's traditional claims.

Tensions mounted over a long-standing dispute between Great Britain and the United States regarding the exact location of the international boundary between the two nations. The political and economic implications were massive. Both nations postured for possession of the prized San Juan Islands. When American farmer Lyman Cutler killed a British pig, just up the way from the lagoon, each side stubbornly entrenched. Armed conflict seemed inevitable.

In July of 1859, Captain George Pickett, 9th U.S. Army Infantry, came ashore at Griffin Bay with sixty-four troops and established a tent camp. A crude sketch was made by a midshipman aboard Her Britannic Majesty's Ship (HBMS) *Satellite* that was also anchored in the bay. It showed the encampment, a dock, and a wagon road up the hill to the ridge and ultimately to Belle Vue Sheep Farm, but not the lagoon. A painting by James Madison Alden (junior officer aboard the US Survey ship *Active* and official artist for the Boundary Survey) from a west-to-east perspective clearly shows the lagoon and San Juan Village, which sprang up on the southeast shoreline.

San Juan Town, as it was later named, was a thriving community and the first permanent settlement on the island. Local historian Mike Vouri has written eloquently about this era in several books including *The Pig War*. He notes that most of the structures at the town were barged in from the abandoned miners' camp on Bellingham Bay following the bust of the Fraser River gold rush. Vouri continues: "Pickett described it as, 'a perfect bedlam day and night.' Prostitutes, murderers, gamblers, sellers of bogus real estate, and all manner of thieves and scalawags came and went."

During The Pig War, the town remained a lively gathering place for commerce and for socializing among islanders and the military. The conflict was peacefully resolved in 1872 by an international commission with Kaiser Wilhelm I of Germany acting as arbitrator. Once America took possession of the island, things changed. First, the British military force left, and then the American contingent. The HBC also retreated. The land began its formal transition to European-American islander-owned agricultural land via the Homestead Act and other commerce. A fire ravaged the Old Town site and it was not rebuilt.

As one would expect, the populating of the Griffin Bay shoreline around Old Town Lagoon was disadvantageous to the pre-settlement wolves. Entries in the *Journal of Charles Griffin* (chief agent for the Hudson's Bay Company) testify to the killing of several wolves due to sheep predation, but likely "the scalawags" also took their toll on the carnivores. The wolves soon disappeared.

~

I continued scanning the lagoon. Its situation, adjacent to the protected bay, spoke to its economic and military values of the past. There are scant reports of the wildlife of that era at this specific spot other than from post reports and Charles Griffin's journal so we are left to guess about the species that called this place home long ago.

There was a green zone that separated me from the muddy substrate. This was the realm of American glasswort (*Salicornia virginica*) that was growing in low, dense mats along the shoreline surrounding the lagoon. It is the signature plant of this tidal habitat with succulent, jointed stems, scaly leaves, and miniscule pinkish-purple flowers that looked like clusters of fiery matchsticks that curiously lured the bees.

The plant's name comes from the Latin for "salty." Its dense structure makes it a useful shelter for small marine invertebrates like crabs that reside in this realm—and today might be food for the avocet. The sheer mass of this plant might suggest a conspicuous presence but *Salicornia* was surprisingly unassuming among the grasses and drift.

Some patches of *Salicornia* at Old Town had been parasitized by saltmarsh dodder, (*Cuscuta salina*) a wiry, orange, filament-like organism that engulfed the pickleweed. The dodder has neither roots nor chlorophyll of its own and depends on *Salicornia* to thrive. The patches of slender orange threads were bright brushstrokes along the drab, muddy shore.

My first acquaintance with dodder was during a field class on seashore life with Dr. Eugene Kozloff, renowned zoologist of the University of Washington Friday Harbor Labs back in the late-1990s. Koz brought us to Jakle's Lagoon—just down the way from Old Town—to see the classic coastal site. He made special note of the dodder that shown bright orange over *Salicornia* in the mud and emphasized its short life as an independent plant after seed germination. As always, any teaching with Koz—and his earnest "Stick to me like a wet shirt" principle—stayed with a student for a lifetime. And so it was on that day, so long ago and fondly remembered.

I glanced right and spied two purplish copper butterflies on the sturdy green stalks of *Salicornia*. Their light tan forms were spattered with tiny flecks of charcoal, bright orange zigzags accentuating hind wings. The coppers were mating—quivering slightly as they went about the business of creating a new generation of gossamer-winged butterflies that would live their entire lives at the lagoon. The orange zigzag pattern on the insect's wings perfectly matched the squiggles of orange dodder—ideal camouflage in this cryptic world of predators and prey.

No cattails at this wetland but plenty of seashore saltgrass, Baltic rush, common rush, slough sedge and seashore fiddleneck.

While still waiting for the avocet to wake up, I turned my back on the lagoon and looked upon the broad, flat expanse of inland sea tagged Ontario Roads, San Juan Harbor, Bellevue Harbor, and Grande Bay before being renamed in honor of Charles Griffin in

September 1854. That 1859 watercolor by Alden depicts a land and seascape that looks remarkably similar today including the towering presence of Mt. Baker in the background. Footings of the old Hudson's Bay Company dock can still be seen at extreme low tides.

A small raft of surf scoters was resting on the slack tide while early eared grebes and horned grebes deep dived for fish in the fertile fjord. Harbor seals snorted boisterously from Half-tide Rocks. Then, as if on cue, a common loon offered one high, trembling call that rippled through the warm air—a stirring refrain from the far north that cast a momentary spell over us all.

My attention was abruptly drawn back to the lagoon as a red fox emerged from the upland woods onto the far edge of the flats. The sun caught the sheen of its lustrous red coat nearly setting it on fire. It was on the prowl, earnestly tiptoeing on spindly black legs and feet across the mud—head down, golden eyes fixed on the substrate, and a long muzzle twitching for a scent. The gadwalls froze. The killdeers ranted. The avocet woke up, pumped its head three times, looked around, then went back to sleep. The fox started when a flock of twelve mallards came screaming in close. It moved into the tall grass, the white tip of its grizzled black tail the only betrayal of its lingering presence. Later a mature bald eagle, white head gleaming, appeared over the lagoon, broad, dark wings held flat in glide mode. The eagle scanned the saltwater through dark, hungry eyes. The avocet did not budge. The bald flew on.

Still later, a sleek river otter appeared out of a snowberry thicket adjacent to July Beach and lumbered hunchbacked over the cobbles to the bay for some fishing. It foraged just offshore using its long, sinuous tail as a rudder to stay on course for Jakle's Lagoon. After several shallow dives, it surfaced, grasping and then munching a crab. The avocet remained unfazed by the noisy otter.

The river otter's behavior reminded me of a time many years before when I had been sitting on a remote beach off Sheep Bay in Prince William Sound, Alaska taking a shore break from surveying sea otters. It was a glorious summer afternoon. I was happy for some time alone after a busy morning with the project crew. The silence was stunning. Bald eagles made lush circles in a cloudless sky. Blackberries were ripening in nearby thickets. I had been counseled by Fish and Wildlife biologist Ancel Johnson to be wary of black bears in the brush and to listen carefully for the slightest indication they were near. As I sat on the sandy beach, I heard a puzzling crunching noise offshore. It took just an instant to realize I was listening to sea otters cracking crab. For a moment, it was the only sound in the Universe. I was humbled at my good fortune to be there—not unlike being at July Beach for this latest crab fest. And, yes, the bears Ancel had warned me about were nearby, but so busy with the berries that they paid me little mind.

~

There was a gentle flow to the afternoon as wildlife and the tide moved in and out to the rhythm of the inland sea. The sun finally disappeared over the far ridge by the Redoubt and with it the warmth of the day. The avocet resumed feeding at the far end of the lagoon, sweeping its curvaceous, black bill back and forth in the water picking up tiny bits of crustacean and insect larvae.

Finally, reluctantly, about half past five o'clock, I bid adieu to the avocet. It was hard to turn away from the spellbinding bird. I took one last look from the trailhead as I left. The avocet was still mining the muck at the lagoon taking long, purposeful strides through the neon green securing its fill through the long daylight hours.

The next morning, I returned to the lagoon hoping to see the brilliant bird once more. There was no trace of the avocet. I walked down the beach to Jakle's Lagoon. No luck there. I suspected it was pointless to launch a wider search. The avocet was gone. I wondered, of course, what happened to the solitary shorebird? What brought it to the islands? Was it a first-year bird that had been separated from the flock migrating north to its breeding grounds and missed the right turn at the Columbia River that would have taken it through the gorge to eastern Washington? Or, perhaps it had lost its mate and, without the flock, did not have a memory map to see it home. Either way, the beautiful bird was on its life's journey—one precarious moment at a time.

So often, as birders, we are lucky to get even a glimpse at some rare or out of range species. Here, I spent the afternoon with one of America's most stunning aviators. That may seem like a long time to sit and watch a shorebird making its way in the world, but there was lots to ponder at the lagoon: how the drift line had changed since last winter's storms; how the warm weather was affecting the evaporation of the lagoon and thus the foraging opportunities for birds; how the feisty red-eyed killdeer were doing; and what must it have been like as grey wolves prowled this shoreline ages ago when the island was still a true wilderness and the predators' howls reverberated across these dark waters, haunting the silences. I wondered, as well, about the Indigenous people's presence at this site dating back many thousands of years. The shelter of the bay was likely advantageous as they went about their spring and summer fishing, hunting and gathering of resources for winter on the mainland. What did the wolf's howl mean to them?

I wished the avocet well. I hoped *Recurvirostra americana* would make its way over the mountains to join its kin on the Okanogan, at the Potholes, or wherever its destiny. The bird was not banded, so I would never know.

Sometimes it is okay not to know what happens in these situations—especially when one has no choice. It is the way of Nature, after all. What I did know was that the avocet was clearly charting its own map of the world—as we chart ours—and doing just fine. Can you imagine the stories this undaunted bird had to tell when it reached its destination?

8

KEEPER
OF THE SEASONS

*A northern red-legged frog, living
in a former fern prairie near town,
listened to a Swainson's thrush during
the breeding season. Frog is deeply
connected to voices from the past.*

A warm rain pelted my bedroom window, announcing a mid-July dawn. Peering outside, I could see a silver sheen high in the evergreens as first light caught the soft drops plummeting to the parched understory. Birds chanted joyful songs. A female rufous hummingbird luxuriated in the shower from her perch on ocean spray, fluffing and combing the iridescent, salal green feathers on her back with her slender bill. The leaf-strewn duff soaked up the storm. I imagined an earthborn sigh of relief that our long dry spell had come to an end. The sharp scent of wet red cedar infused the air like a blessing offered to the sky for the good fortune of an island rain.

~

I had been waiting for the drought to pass to go looking for red-legged frogs. Why frogs? For a naturalist, the question might rather be, why not? They are intriguing animals, not always easy to find. While fairly common in some coastal areas in the Pacific Northwest, they were not believed to be common in the San Juans. Each island has its own unique fauna. Few surveys for the frogs had been done here, and their status was unknown.

I had found a red-legged frog only once—by chance—in a forest not far from my home. It had been a brief, but charming, encounter. I was eager to find Frog again, and knew just the secluded spot to search. Successful or not, the quest would be fun. Meandering among towering conifers, mysterious (to me) mushrooms, irascible woodpeckers, and the last of the summer breeding birds suited me perfectly.

The rain ensured conditions would be perfect for the search. The early hour was appropriate as the Latin name for the species (*Rana aurora aurora*) is "aurora" meaning sunrise. I headed out to greet the day and hopefully this intriguing amphibian.

It can be challenging to find frogs in the dappled woods. Picture a moist, mature forest primarily Douglas fir with western cedar, shore pine, a smattering of western hemlock, and an understory of sword ferns, Oregon grape and salal. Add a meandering creek and you have the ideal island habitat for red-legged frogs. They are small——only about three to five inches long. Aurora exemplifies Nature's perfect camouflage: a body richly patterned in shades of gold, black, rusty-red and light brown to blend into a world of leaf litter and tangles of woody debris along a muddy wetland. The disruptive coloration is its best defense against predators that include raccoons, fox, heron and garter snakes. The frogs are easily recognized by a dark mask, light jawline strip, a prominent fold from their eye strip along the side, and a pinkish to reddish wash over their lower abdomen and underside of their hind legs.

These are endearing creatures: wide-eyed, patient beings that sit mindfully like little Buddhas in the rain shadows contemplating the chorus of woodland songs that define their habitat, and earnestly unfolding their sticky tongues to snatch insects that whirl by. Snatching those bugs is important. The "red-legs"—one of two native species in the islands—are stewards of the forest helping to ensure balance by devouring massive numbers of insects.

There is a rich mythology connected to red-legged frogs and Pacific tree (chorus) frogs. Coast Salish lore tells us the chorus frog—

smaller, louder and more demonstrative than its kin—proclaims the renewal that comes with spring. At dusk and into the night, the frogs sing their mating songs and, in so doing, affirm the end to the longhouse season of winter for Indigenous people and a reconnection to the hunting, fishing and gathering times about to begin.

Frog is also the messenger, the communicator who travels between the two worlds of land and water both naturally and supernaturally. There is great power in its transformation—from egg to tadpole to adult. This brings knowledge and awareness that Frog shares with other forest dwellers. Great reverence has been given to this amphibian as demonstrated in Indigenous art and culture. I liked the idea of Frog as mystic, and had my own suspicions about its powers of perception.

The pebbled gray sky was a welcome change from Salish blue. The rain increased the possibility of finding Aurora. As it turned out, my search did not take long. Once in the woods, an overturned trail plant's arrowhead-shaped leaf shone silver at my feet pointing the way down the trail. I startled a red-legged frog perched beside a sword fern in the duff. It made one short leap to stay out of my way then settled in the greenery looking up at me looking down at its charming, masked face. Dare I suggest it had an inscrutable smile?

I was delighted to find Frog. I bent down to take a photograph fearing it would quickly disappear. It watched me through golden eyes the color of a spent red cedar bough and obliged me by sitting still. We had a momentary faceoff, assessing one another, before I withdrew to give it space. As a nocturnal species, Frog was understandably quiet now and I did not want to disturb its rest. Nightfall would come soon enough. I was sorry to miss its more active time, but I stayed a while watching and admiring the frog and listening to the many voices of the forest.

Years before, I named this place Creeper's Woods as a reference in my field journals. I found my first brown creeper's nest tucked into a cavity behind a loose piece of bark on a very old, fire-scarred Douglas fir just down the trail. One morning, as mist sifted through the canopy, I noticed an adult creeper—a tiny brown perching bird with a wing span just over four inches—flying to and fro the crevice with grubs and knew there must be chicks inside. I watched and waited for several days and finally Behold! Three brand new creepers appeared on the trunk of the nest tree. They were replicas of the adults with mottled brown feathers above and white below–the perfect abstraction of tree bark. They cheeped and fluttered their wings in that baby bird way of asking for food, but quickly took up the task of foraging on their own in the deep folds of the fir. They sang a thin, high-pitched series of call notes famed ornithologist and illustrator David Sibley characterizes as "trees, trees, pretty little trees" while earnestly working up the trunk, then spiraling down—sort of. They were still learning and started again nudging their tiny decurved bills into the creases of wood and smatterings of light blue-green lichen for spiders and other insects and eggs. The tree hugging fledglings used stiff tails—woodpecker style—to steady themselves as they mined the bark. That first morning of flight, the woods seemed to belong to the creepers.

It was still early as I kept company with Frog. Many of the birds were quiet but the air vibrated with the Swainson's thrushes fluting song, the olive-sided flycatcher's staccato "quick-three-beers," the beeping of nuthatches, and a Pacific-slope flycatcher, always the ventriloquist, calling *pee-u-weet* from the depths of the shadowy green. Wrens ranted, a handsome towhee trilled, and a flock of juvenile chickadees noisily worked on their foraging skills. The small creek fifty footsteps below my post—the outfall from Beaverton Valley just up the way—had nearly dried up and struggled to emit even a soft gurgle in the mud on its watery way to a kingfisher cove near town. The bright pink inflorescence of tall, lean Cooley's hedge nettle added exclamation points along the banks of the stream.

Woodland (broad-leaved) starflower and Linnaeus's beloved twin-flower, tiny elegant ivory blooms of late spring, were going to seed. There were woodchips everywhere from the excavations of a pileated woodpecker that occasionally took up its rapid-fire drumbeat while I sat under the canopy.

Aurora was a fine frog. One might say an illusionist. When I looked away to check on some chattering birds, I struggled to find the earth-toned amphibian again when I glanced back so perfect was its concealment by the ferns. Each aspect of its coloration was assimilated to the setting: the blotched tan back mimicking bark and dried leaves, and dark stripes and mask as disruptive patterns in the maze of sticks, stones, leaves and bark. While nothing is truly invisible in the forest if one looks closely enough, Aurora was being supremely inconspicuous—part of Frog's magic, perhaps.

A slight breeze riffed the serrated sword ferns fanning Frog. After a few minutes it grew more relaxed and changed position. At one point, Aurora rose a bit on its partially webbed toes as if straining to hear something and then settled back down. It was always on watch perceiving life in the woods I could barely imagine.

I had questions for the red-legged frog. I wondered how far it would roam from the relative safety of the creek. Perhaps up the way where the white fawn lilies dwelled. The pristine blooms had gone to seed—their inflorescence transformed into four-sided pods that would soon release to the forest floor next year's promise for another wildflower spring in this dappled green world. There were remnants of camas and chocolate lilies, too, harkening back to the time of the plants being tended by Indigenous people.

I was curious about how Frog would survive the winter. Who were its allies? It was a short, one-sided conversation. I did not linger with Aurora, though. Even from a distance, using binoculars, I feared stressing the frog. Surely, that would be no kindness for the gift of appearance it had given me.

~

Fern prairie. It was easy to take this forest for granted, so formidable were the trees and so entrenched and entwined the vegetation—as if it had always been there. But, as with other woodlands on San Juan Island, that was not the case.

Actually, this patch of mature conifers is on the fringe of shoreline property once designated as a "fern prairie." Maps from an 1874 survey by the U.S. General Land Office indicate a broad swath of territory from the south-facing slope of Point Caution as "... open land covered with bracken and grasses ..." The land was occupied for a time by a rancher named Thomas McCarty who raised sheep there. It was designated a military reservation in the late 1800s. In 1921, 476 acres were transferred to the University of Washington and became the Friday Harbor Laboratories Biological Preserve.

Biologist Dr. Tom Schroeder did exhaustive research on the site and reported: "... that for at least five hundred years, until about a century ago, the site was a coastal prairie composed of grasses, bracken and wildflowers and maintained by Native people; scattered across the prairie were a few widely separated, open-grown Douglas-firs, some of which survive today as wolf trees in the modern forest ..."

Historical photographs taken from Friday Harbor clearly show a significantly different landscape than we know today, the open habitat now surrounded by dense forest and home to red-legged frogs and an entire complex web of woodland dwellers.

How was the prairie maintained against the encroachment of conifers all those years? The ancient history of that place has not, to date, been retrieved but, as Schroeder comments:

"... it seems reasonable to assume that Native people kept it open with periodic, low-intensity burning from at least A.D. 1400 to 1850 ... such indigenous people presumably managed the prairie in order to exploit edible bulbs of the sun-loving camas and chocolate lily, whose few descendants still bloom on Point Caution's sunny, moss-covered outcrops of bedrock …"

Later, without burning or sheep grazing the land reverted to a Douglas fir woodland. That modern forest has retained its wild, if disheveled, character over the last century and has gone largely unmanaged. The forest succession is a classic example of how landscapes change over time.

~

The rain subsided so I wandered down to the creek. On the way, I found the feather of a northern flicker. The woods supported several flicker families—members of the woodpecker clan. I was hearing the *yuk-yuk-yuk* calls of the newly fledged juveniles as they flitted from tree trunk to tree trunk chiseling, hammering at the bark with their long, dark bills, and displaying boundless curiosity about their surroundings. They seemed to play peek-a-boo with one another as they flung themselves on brand new salmon-colored wings with remarkable agility through the dense woods.

I picked up the feather—a small, round-tipped secondary. It was tannish with a bright salmon shaft; rows of creamy spots at the edges were etched in the shape of little hearts. I wondered what the significance was of that design. Surely the hearts had some role to play in camouflage or communication.

Nearby, a pine white butterfly had fallen prey to a spider and was entangled in its web. While I was sorry to see the pristine beauty hopelessly bound, still it illustrated the interwoven nature of this forest.

Then there was the ten-lined June bug—actually a scarab beetle—I unearthed from the leaf litter with my boot. What an appealing armored being: peppered russet-gray above with large white stripes along its wing covers. June bugs feed on foliage, mostly at night. I had dislodged this one at rest and received its strident call as an admonition—part hissing and part saw-like stridulation (rubbing its wings together). I felt badly for the disturbance and offered my apologies.

At the creek, water was barely flowing. Once-deep pools of cool runoff from the valley above were now mostly mud puddles. Raccoons, deer and fox ventured to this spot early each morning for fresh water. I suspected that tadpoles had already metamorphosed into those red-legged frogs, as there was no haven to be found in the stream by summer.

I was reminded that it was in this exact spot only weeks before where I had encountered a Pacific treefrog. I was sitting on a log watching echo azure butterflies fluttering about blooming lance-leaved stonecrop near the shore. Out of the corner of my eye I saw a movement in the duff. Peering through the foliage I spied the tiny, bright green frog. It knew I was there and was clearly headed for deeper cover. The caroler took only a moment to look me in the eye, then leaped into a labyrinth of salal—perfect camouflage. The shy soul did not make a sound. I was pleased to know that both species of our native frogs were using the slow-moving stream in Creeper's Woods.

Before I left for home, I checked on *Rana aurora aurora* again. It was still nearby in the shade of an old cedar stump that was playing its role in the undergrowth by acting as a nurse log for seedlings. Frog peered at me with knowing eyes and held its ground.

I paused and listened to the Swainson's thrush's poignant call again, perhaps for the last time before the olive-backed bird headed south, migrating possibly as far as Central America. The refrain floated high through the conifers. It was like an ancient song symbolizing the wildness that still exists—if greatly diminished—in the islands. I looked at Aurora to see if it was standing high on its little lobed feet listening as it had done earlier in the day. I wished it to be so.

I will rejoice in the Swainson's return next spring with its gift of luxurious song when the salmonberry begins bearing fruit. I suspect that Aurora will be waiting and listening, too. The keeper of the seasons may have stories to share with Thrush about winter in these woods and goings-on we humans cannot begin to imagine. Yes, a frog with secrets.

Hundreds of years ago, this place was a prairie. Now, it is a forest. It will change again. The First People understood Frog's presence here was important to them and to the other creatures of this realm. Listening to the voices of the past and honoring that wisdom is a good thing.

9

ONE SMALL PATCH

A woodland skipper nectared on pearly everlasting on an island grassland. The unassuming wildflower is a beacon for late summer butterflies.

Sometimes, under a great expanse of sky, there appear small treasures on the landscape that require a closer look. And so it was with a patch of glistening white plants I found years ago growing wild along a roughshod road that split an island prairie into fragments of tall grass and rabbit warrens.

The plants were pearly everlasting—hundreds of them—growing in a fifteen by twenty-foot square plot surrounded by golden prairie grasses. The statuesque plants stood three feet tall with small, paper-thin blooms—ivory bracts with modest yellow stamens sitting atop slender celery-green stalks shining silver in the light. They projected a pristine aura as if they had come into flower all at once—and not long before. "Here we are," they seemed to say. It took me a moment to understand what that meant.

Oh, I had seen pearly everlasting before on the island, a common species of meadows, fields, rocky slopes and open woodlands, but the plants had never made a lasting impression. Maybe the difference was that this patch was full of tiny butterflies. The lure was irresistible.

I stopped, of course, to look more closely and discovered nearly two-dozen woodland skipper butterflies feeding on the ivory blooms. The small, tawny tribe—each less than one inch across—worked methodically through the stately plants keying on the yellow centers of the globe-like flowers. The butterflies were having a feast drawing sugar from the floral nectarines with their long, fine proboscises. I watched one skipper, when finished feeding, curl its agile tool out of sight against its face—an almost magical feat of "Now you see it; now you don't." They did not start when I bent down to admire them.

I have a fondness for skippers. They are endearing insects. The skippers earnestly dart about the scape and, when perched with wings open, look a bit like tiny jet planes with fiery orange and gold airfoils landing on a cushion of soft blooms. They are perhaps best known to island gardeners who find them on lavender and other late blooming plants. I referred to the elfins in the patch as "Skippy" and knew I would be returning to see how these seemingly lighthearted souls were doing, and to identify some of the other visitors to this sunny realm.

Pearly everlasting has been admired by botanists and naturalists since early exploration of North America. Its scientific name is *Anaphalis margaritacea*. In Greek, "ana" means upward, above or high upon, and "phalos" shining white. Margaritacea is from the Latin Margarits for "pearl" or "pearl-like." Thus, we have a shining white, pearl-like flower with the typical composite structure of the Asteraceae (sunflowers).

I checked several botany guides looking for details or impressions of the plant. Ship's naturalist Archibald Menzies catalogued *A. margaritacea* during George Vancouver's Voyage of Discovery that plied through Northwest waters in 1792.

Henry David Thoreau wrote in his journal of the plant's September presence: "… it is dry and unwithering … its amaranthine quality is instead of high color … an imaginary flower that never fades." As such, some folks cut and hang pearly everlasting upside down to dry and, as it retains its color and texture, the flowers become beautiful, long-lasting bouquets.

I read Thoreau's description in Mrs. William Starr Dana's book *How to Know the Wild Flowers*, first published in 1893. I had come across a tattered copy of the book at a local library sale years before and been intrigued by the work of the early self-taught naturalist who, after her first husband died, remarried and went by the name Francis Theodora Parsons. The book was heralded as the first field guide to North American wildflowers—an instant success. Both Theodore Roosevelt and Rudyard Kipling voiced praise for her work. Following *Wildflowers*, Starr Dana (Parsons) wrote *According to Season* (1894) and *Plants and their Children* (1896). Then, as Parsons, *How to Know the Ferns* in 1899. Engaging books all. I am grateful to pearly everlasting for encouraging my revisiting Starr Dana's legacy. She was one of America's best early women naturalists.

~

In pre-European settlement of the islands, pearly everlasting had a rich cultural role with the First People. The Coast Salish frequented this very spot, now known as American Camp. Each spring and summer six thousand or more years ago, they fished off South Beach, collected mollusks and shellfish, hunted fowl, cultivated camas, and gathered provisions for winter. Indigenous people knew this plant well. Pillows and mattresses were stuffed with the hardy flowers; an infusion of the entire plant was used to wash wounds; the blooms were also employed to make a tea that combated asthma; rubbing the plant on one's hands softened them; and folklore tells us it was mixed into a salve for burns. Do you suppose the butterflies were here then, too?

~

I returned to that patch of pearly everlasting every summer. It was tucked up against the Redoubt, but the plant was not showy elsewhere on the grassland. One afternoon, I wondered to con-servation biologist Dr. Amy Lambert, while we chatted at South Beach, why there was so little of this plant on the plain. I still commonly found it along the drift line at the beach and elsewhere. She had been checking on pearly everlasting, too, and knew of two large patches down the hill west of the Redoubt. Amy suggest-ed these remnant beds might be holdouts from early agricultural times when the fields were cleared of stones; seeds may have been lodged in the rocky outcrops where they continued to flourish—protected from the plows.

Woodland skippers were not the only butterflies that visited *Anaphalis margaritacea* here. I sat sometimes on the split rail fence nearby to observe the comings and goings in the patch. One late August morning under an azure sky unencumbered by clouds, I was joined by a pair of red-tailed hawks making circular sweeps over-head, a family of California quail scurrying across the road into Nootka rose, goldfinch bouncing through the thin air on their way to a thistle feast, and cedar waxwings gorging on crab apple fruit up the way. The grasshopper chorus was in full voice.

The plants were lush, growing closely together, and very showy that year. They beckoned. In thirty minutes, five skippers visited the clusters of white button-like heads. They stayed a long time.

Another grassland dweller, the ochre (common) ringlet, was nec-taring on the blooms, too. Like the skippers, the ringlets are earth-toned textured; hues of light cinnamon and deer-hide gray create an aura of invisibility for the butterfly on the plain. They are bigger—about one and a half inches—and rounder than the angular-shaped skippers, and more subdued. The nymphs produce soft flutters out of the grass as they foraged. It is not always a good survival strategy, though; I have seen them snatched in midair by pipits migrating south across the scape in September. The web of life here works hard keeping its balance.

As I continued to watch, a grasshopper, armored in mustard green and gold, sprang on stripy, orange pins aboard one of the blooms for a rest; a fat humblebee snoozed in the stalks; and a variegated meadowhawk (dragonfly)—looking every bit like the ancient soul it was—levitated over the patch before zooming off to catch the air currents that always seemed to swirl around an old broken-topped Douglas fir that incubated insects for hungry airborne prowlers.

A pair of purplish copper butterflies touched down in the pearly-white stand and began feeding. The female was brown and bright orange above with black spots and brown borders. The males appeared, at first glance, a more subtle pinkish tan, but when the light brushed his body just so, a blue-violet, almost lilac, hue refracted from the scaly surface of its wings that softly shimmered. The contract between the two coppers was stark—a demonstration of the role color plays in their attraction and mating.

Renowned lepidopterist and author Robert Michael Pyle, who spent considerable time on San Juan Island in the early 2000s doing butterfly surveys, wrote of the purplish copper: "The butterfly is one of the great survivors ... watchers will enjoy the Purplish Copper almost everywhere, often as a member of a tough gang of highly adaptive species including the Mylitta Crescent and Woodland Skipper. Together they help keep western Washington from being completely butterfly-free." Indeed, the only member of this gang that was missing was the Mylitta crescent, once common here but hard to find in recent times. I knew from spending time with Bob in the field that his observations are keen and his devotion to butterflies unbounded.

The morning warmed into the 70s. I hesitated to leave and wondered what I might miss by walking away from the patch too soon. I knew the American lady used pearly everlasting as both a host plant and a nectar source. I've only seen The Lady on San Juan once, thanks to the acute observations of islanders Eleanor and Kurt Mc-Millan who spied one at Cattle Point many years before and were kind enough to share the sighting. Perhaps late summer ladies stop here, too, but prefer their privacy.

And, red admirals were nearby, as well. I saw them frequently in late summer and early fall, making brief stops at the patch amidst their energetic fluttering about the plain. One late October, I watched dozens of admirals migrating past this spot on their way south. It was the thrilling discovery of an event not documented before at the park. I wrote about it in *Rainshadow World.*

Alas, it was time to go. I wanted to catch up with those goldfinch I had seen earlier seeking thistle stands for seed to fuel their journeys south.

It had been fun watching pearly everlasting maintaining its place on the plain, but time was taking its toll. Hawthorn, snowberry, blackberry, non-native grasses, and bracken were making inroads into the rocky, lichen-laden flower bed. The split rail fence had been torn down, and black-tailed deer had forged a trail through the heart of the stately stalks allowing hikers a new shortcut to the shore. The changes bothered me. I worried that this feeding station for the butterflies might be in jeopardy. Certainly, the loss of one patch of pearly everlasting would not be of critical significance to wildlife but the cumulative effect of fragmentation would eventually matter. I had seen it happen elsewhere.

I reached down to pull out an especially large hawthorn volunteer that was entwining the everlasting. Surely a little "tending" would do no harm. Then, I remembered a quote by English Poet Francis Thompson: "... Thou canst not stir a flower without troubling of a star ..." I paused. The sentiment was not lost on me. There was far more going on biologically in that patch than I would ever dream of understanding. Sometimes doing the right thing means doing nothing.

So, I bid adieu to the pearly everlasting and to the clan of butter-flies for another season. By the time the shrikes and meadowlarks arrived for the winter, the steadfast plants would have lost their lus-ter. From glimmering white to a weary sepia, the flowers would fade into fall on this salt-sprayed, wind-swept plain. The next generation of butterflies (eggs and larvae) was likely already settled in the grass until next spring. I suspected, as I went about my winter rounds near the Redoubt, I might stop occasionally at the patch just to see how things were going.

10
LONG-DISTANCE DRAGONS

A variegated meadowhawk paused on the prairie during fall migration through the island. Sometimes several thousand dragons appeared in a single day.

Who was that? I said to myself. Several small, dark figures zoomed in front of my windshield as I drove over the rise at Pickett's Lane headed for South Beach. It was six o'clock. Sunset was two hours away. At the height of fall migration, I had spent the early September afternoon looking for mixed flocks of birds that surged through the islands on their way south after the breeding season. It had not been a productive day except for the ruby-crowned kinglets and hermit thrushes I found foraging at the willow grove at Cattle Point. I was tired, disappointed, and thinking of heading home. Well, maybe one last stop along the prairie to make sure I was not missing anything.

I had been spoiled over time watching migrating birds and butterflies on the island. Flocks of thousands of shorebirds swirled through the morning mist at False Bay. Dozens of red admiral butterflies surged into the clouds and away from the shoreline by the lighthouse at Cattle Point. Savannah sparrows, by the hundreds, sought shelter from a rainstorm in a huge thistle patch at the dunes. Masses of barn swallows staged above the grasslands before heading out. A Douglas fir crammed full of roosting turkey vultures taking a break at Jakle's Woods while hopscotching their way down the coast from the Gulf Islands once caught my eye. Thrushes, larks, bluebirds, terns, pipits, several species of warblers, flycatchers and vireos passed through. I loved them all, but true to my naturalist's core I was always wondering what else was just down the trail. Oh, how I loved September!

∼

Those wiry, dark forms that whirred in front of the car were dragonflies. I knew that much for sure, but was surprised to see them together—half a dozen flying only a few feet apart. Several yards down Pickett's Lane more of the slender forms sped by. I pulled off the lane by the split rail fence to get a better perspective scrambling from my car with binoculars in hand. It took only a few moments, looking north and west, to realize that dozens—no, hundreds at least—of dragons were flying, in loose formation, just above the prairie grass heading south. I had come upon a migration event.

There was nobody around. A hint of easterly breeze was moving across Haro Strait from the Pacific. The sun hovered over Vancouver Island shining through a gathering of buttermilk clouds crowding the blue sky that stretched toward Canada. The heat of the day was dwindling, but this was no time for a weather report.

I was stunned. The surge was impressive—only the second time I had witnessed mass numbers of dragonflies on the move. It looked like a scene from a science fiction film with hoards of alien-like beings headed right at me. I took a deep breath. This was an important occurrence. My awe would have to wait. What do I do first?

Dragonflies were not my forte and identification skills were nil. The only reason I so quickly keyed on the phenomenon was because of an event I had witnessed at Cape May, New Jersey some years before.

∼

I had travelled to the eastern shore on a birding and butterfly excursion with my sister Jan. It was early fall. We were especially keen on seeing the monarch migration, but it was not a good year for *Danaus plexippus*. We were mourning the low numbers of iconic butterflies over lunch at the Ocean View Restaurant off the boardwalk. Sitting at a window table, we noticed hundreds of dragonflies whirring down Main Street and along the shore. Locals seated nearby were paying no attention to them. I asked our waitress what was going on. She commented nonchalantly that the dragonflies were passing through on migration.

We continued to see dragons during the next few days on our monarch forays. Local naturalist and Cape May Observatory program director Pat Sutton told us they were black saddlebag dragonflies—a regular visitor at the shore each fall. We got excellent looks at perched *Tramea lacerata* while taking class with Pat. The dragons were stout at two inches long: overall very dark brown or blackish, dark eyes, and had dark patches at the bases of their hind wings, giving them their common name. There was no doubt they had saddlebags. We saw thousands of them during our stay. The experience was an excellent primer on dragonfly migration and a foreshadowing of what was to come on San Juan Island years later.

~

The dragons were flying low and fast around me at Pickett's, single-mindedly going south. They changed course to avoid hitting me. Could I get photographs? No! Too many. Too small. Flying too fast.

I must document this, I thought, but how? Keeping it simple, I marked off several sections of split rail fence along the road as reference points and began counting as the dragons crossed within that boundary.

In one minute, one hundred dragons flew across the fence line. In five minutes, my count was over five hundred. At the half hour mark, several thousand dragonflies had sped past me. I took a break. My head was spinning. The insects were moving so fast I feared I was not grasping the magnitude of the event. I got back into my car and drove the length of the lane to assess the situation as the stream continued. There were dragonflies as far as I could see from the shoreline to Redoubt Road. The numbers were staggering.

Time hurtled by as quickly as the flyers. I went back to my original vantage point, checked the time, and kept counting. I was the only person there. No other cars. No walkers. Had I stepped into the Twilight Zone? No, but I needed to find someone to confirm the sightings. There was no cell phone service at the shore so I would have to take a break. Who was nearby? Ah, my pal, conservation biologist and author Thor Hanson would be perfect, and he was just up the way.

I sped up Cattle Point Road to Thor and Eliza's place, pulled into the driveway and spotted Thor down by the Raccoon Shack where he had his office. All smiles, as usual, he was quick to rally when I gave him the news, grabbing his binoculars as he jumped in his car and followed me back to the park.

Well over an hour had passed since my initial encounter with the swarm. The light was beginning to fade as we reached the lane. The stream was slowing but still there were many dozens of dragons powering by. I took a net from the trunk of my car and gave it to Thor. He nabbed a dragon on his first swing. Here was our chance for identification—maybe. Thor carefully placed the prize in a specimen jar—required equipment for an occasional catch and release of small insects (especially butterflies, dragons and bees) for identification or relocation out of harm's way. What a beauty! It was medium-sized for a dragon: a long, segmented abdomen with a pattern of gray, yellow, and burnt orange; whitish abdominal spots;

and two prominent white stripes and yellow spots on each side of the thorax. I did not know what species it was. Thor had his suspicions but was not ready to make a definitive call. I took photographs and would make a positive identification later.

Clouds were gathering. Dusk was descending over the grassland. Thor had to get home. Before he left, we released the dragon back to the prairie and watched it whir away. No harm done. Thor and I exchanged wide grins and enthusiastic chatter about our unexpected encounter before he headed out with my thanks for the assist.

The last rays of the sun were losing their sheen. A few dragons continued passing through. Dozens more dropped into the grass on the north side of the road choosing hairy cat's ear, an aster considered by many an invasive weed, as their roosting site for the night. Some also held fast to nipplewort. Sometimes, three or four of the weary insects gathered on the same plant, grasping the stems with their minute steel-blue legs. As a golden afterglow settled across the plain, the migrants succumbed to the evening chill and were still. They appeared vulnerable, but darkness would protect them from predatory birds, especially migrating kestrels, that could be a threat during the day. In the last scattering of light, the dragons' delicate multi-colored bodies and clear outspread wings glistened like gold in the grass.

Just before darkness fell, I spied an ochre ringlet butterfly, a resident of the park. It was clad in shades of cinnamon and gold with a lightning bolt of cream across its hindwing—in perfect harmony with the muted tones of the scape. The tiny nymph settled in the grass with the dragons. Come morning, I was not sure if it would be peer or prey for the dragons.

The sky turned midnight blue except for a raspberry-red wash that hung over Haro Strait and dipped into the grass to the northwest. The blaze of color nearly set the plains on fire before the sky went to sleep—a great punctuation mark to end the day. The grasshopper chorus dimmed as the dragons reposed and the little ringlet held fast to its perch.

Darkness came swiftly. A waxing crescent moon did not offer much light. I stood by the fence and listened—not wanting to leave. A calm descended over the plain, like moments of grace blessing the tired travelers. I got my flashlight and walked uphill to Redoubt Road wondering if there were dragons perched in the grass there, too. Yes. I easily found over a dozen in hairy cat's ear by the fence line. I wanted a closer look and more photographs but stumbling about in the dark—possibly disturbing individuals I had not discovered—was clearly not a good idea. Reluctantly, I headed back to Friday Harbor.

At home, I downloaded images from my Nikon, transcribed field notes, and took Dennis Paulson's early work, *Dragonflies of Washington,* from the shelf to identify the species Thor and I had seen. Dragonflies are members of the order Odonata, and are called "odonates." In Greek that means "the toothed ones" although the dragons don't have teeth. They grasp their prey with strong mandibles. Most of the dragons I observed displayed intricate patterns of colors and markings on their long abdomens—perfectly adorned in camouflage colors for the flight of their lives. I found a photograph of variegated meadowhawks, a species description in Paulson's book. Two white strips and two yellow spots on each side of their thorax were diagnostic of immatures. That was it. I did some math and estimated that over eighty thousand meadowhawks had migrated through the park that late afternoon. I had no idea how many pushed through earlier in the day.

I wanted to watch the meadowhawks awakening the next morning to continue their journey, so I set my alarm for five o'clock. Images of golden dragons swirled in my head as I fell asleep.

First light! I hurried back to Pickett's Lane. It was still dark, but a small flock of savannah sparrows was already foraging for insects and seeds on the shoulder of Cattle Point Road. Pink and blue light peaked over Mt. Baker to the east and slowly infused its way across Griffin Bay to the island. Thirty minutes later, the fields began to take on a golden hue as I caught a glimpse of a fat black fox chasing a rabbit into its warren one hundred yards away. I was delighted to have made it back to the park before the next chapter of the saga began.

I found the meadowhawks still clinging to their resting places on the plain. While the chill was quickly dissipating, it was too cold for the insects to fly. I watched and waited for the awakening, walking carefully down a fox trail into the grass to get a closer look at the still stationary sojourners. I snapped a few photos but remained hesitant to intrude upon their rest at such a crucial time. The grass was moist with dew. The dragons glistened. The European rabbits were stirring, too, unfazed by the invasion of the momentary migrators. It was a scene reminiscent perhaps of an earlier time (minus the rabbits) when this plain was called Home Prairie by the Hudson's Bay Company. Did the dragons stop by then, too?

About seven o'clock, the insects began to stir. Their bodies trembled slightly as they warmed up. Then the four wings of a sleek little traveler began to whir and liftoff. Moments later, several of the meadowhawks were airborne just as the sun rose over Cape San Juan.

The first order of the day for *Sympetrum corruptus* was refueling before continuing their journey. Dozens of dragons emerged from the grass. They hunted, perched, basked in the sunlight and then, one by one, headed out. I watched them whir low over the dunes, across the ancient ice fields, and out of sight past the terraced slope of Mt. Finlayson toward Cattle Point. By nine o'clock, most of the meadowhawks were gone. I stood knee-deep in the grass looking for stragglers—for one more dragon to bid adieu and wish a safe journey. For the time being, it was not meant to be.

In the days that followed, I searched the internet for information about dragonfly migration. On September 7, the headlines in Oregon newspapers read: "Dragonflies Swarm Cannon Beach" and "Mass Flights of Dragonflies Create Awe on Oregon Coast." From the Tweeters Birding E-mail site, I learned that hordes of dragonflies had descended on Tokeland, Washington the same day I saw them on San Juan Island. They had been sighted in the vicinity of the Olympic Mountains as well. Some guessed million of meadowhawks had been seen; biologists set the estimate more likely at many hundreds of thousands. Either way, the migration along the Washington and Oregon coastline had been a true phenomenon.

I contacted noted dragonfly expert and author Dr. Dennis Paulson, director emeritus of the University of Puget Sound's Slater Museum of Natural History, whose book I had used to make the identification. He explained that the variegated meadowhawk—one of only a few dragonflies to undertake long-distance migrations—were headed for California and northern Mexico. They were coming from their breeding grounds to the north, in British Columbia. The species is also widespread in the southern part of the Canadian Prairie Provinces, but those individuals may have migrated east of the Rockies. The regional meadowhawks' migration had previously been observed mostly along the outer coast of Washington and Oregon. Paulson reported: "This movement appeared to be more widespread. Observers saw very large flights in the Pasayten wilderness and right out of the Columbia Basin. It was really quite amazing, far more than I have heard of before. Or is it just that more and more people are keyed in to look for them?" Dennis explained that once the meadowhawks get to their destination, they would lay eggs and die leaving their offspring to migrate north again in the spring where the cycle of life will continue.

Dennis was especially pleased to hear of the meadowhawks appearance in the San Juan Islands. It was the first documented sighting in this area. There is still much to understand about the mysterious movements of the meadowhawks. They may appear along the outer coast one day and disappear the next. No one is sure where they go. Easterly winds may have been a factor in pushing them inland to the islands. Dennis concluded: "The meadowhawks are beautiful dragonflies, not fully appreciated because most people only see them from a distance."

I continued to patrol the shortgrass prairie at American Camp for the rest of September looking for more dragons. On September 14, I encountered another surge in late afternoon. This time easily twenty thousand dragonflies passed through within two hours, then it began to rain. It poured all night. The next day they were gone, but every day thereafter, throughout September, I found at least a few of the variegated meadowhawks at the south end. Usually, they were hunting. Sometimes they basked on rocks along the trail. On one occasion, I saw meadowhawks mating, data important to biologists who are still learning about their behavior during migration.

I stayed in touch with Dennis throughout September and had lots of questions for him about meadowhawk behavior. He was quick to oblige my curiosity.

"My guess is they mostly migrate over land, as they would be subject to more winds over water that they might not be able to fight. They may be in big trouble when they get blown out over the Pacific Ocean, as they are certainly not as strong fliers as some of the other migrants. Their presence in the islands certainly indicates they do fly over water, but those are fairly short distances. Unlike common green darners and wandering gliders, which migrate over the Gulf of Mexico in large numbers, this species doesn't seem to make any

long overwater flights. It has been found on offshore California islands in the fall, along with the green darners, but I think mostly
in small numbers.

No one knows where they are coming from, but there are large
numbers in the interior as well, and I would be surprised if any came
over here from east of the Rockies. They breed all over Washington."

I was elsewhere for most of October. Finally, I got back to Redoubt
Road and found three migrants one day, two the next, and then one
lone variegated meadowhawk zoomed into view on October 28. Its
elegant, red, needle-like body darted methodically through soft air
that was starting to get a little rough around the edges snatching
bugs before it whirred out of sight over the ridge. I suspected there
were still a few stragglers in the area, but I found the vision of this
male making its way south alone poignant after having seen such a
magnificent mass of dragons earlier. It was a good way to end my
season with the ancient insects that fossils show us have lived on
earth for nearly three hundred million years.

I was reminded of a phrase by American poet, essayist and gar-
dener Celia Thaxter who lived on one of the Isles of Shoals off
Portsmouth, New Hampshire in the late 1800s. In *Already* (1878),
she wrote: "… O, brief, bright smile of summer! …" and so it was
here on San Juan Island, too, and almost gone.

Now it was fall—time to turn my attention to shrikes, short-eared
owls, kestrels and newly arrived meadowlarks and northern harriers—the winter residents of the plain as the cycle of life continued.
Before making the pivot, though, there was time to ponder beguil-
ing dragons. Was this the first time they had migrated through the
San Juans or had they been passing through, unnoticed, for decades
or even centuries? Where do they go when they disappear for days
at a time during their journeys south? How are changing landscapes and changing climate affecting their movements and their
populations? What role does our grassland play in sustaining the

meadowhawks, the insects they prey upon, and the predators that prey upon them? We have a lot to learn from dragonflies about the intricate ways of the natural world.

Perhaps we could learn from dragonflies how better to navigate our own life journeys. I observed the dragons never looked back, never circled around or went back, stopped to rest when they needed to, made course corrections depending on the events of the day (temperature, wind, cloud cover) and kept moving forward to the very edge of night.

The dragons were living in the moment—giving life everything they had. Every beat of their gilded wings mattered. Their minds were not cluttered by recollections of the past or expectations of the future. They only had now and they made the most of it.

Life according to the variegated meadowhawk. I love these lessons so unexpectedly—and beautifully—delivered.

11
WALKING
WITH PIPITS

*In September and October, gregarious
American pipits stopped along the shoreline
to rest before continuing their flights to
wintering grounds southward. They
might walk part of the way.*

We do not always get what we want in life.
We do not always get as far as we would like to go.
We get as far as we get.
And, if we are lucky, there will be someone there
*   to help us finish our journey,*
Or at least make the end time meaningful.

I wrote those words in my journal about an injured bird I found at the south end of the island on a mist-shrouded morning during fall migration. I spotted the motionless brown form in the road, stopped, grabbed a tissue, got out of my car, and scooped it up. The bird was alive, looked up at me with soft brown eyes, and relaxed into my grasp. It was small and easily fit in the palm of my hand. Its feathers were buffy gray and brown with unfinished edges—an immature. The songbird seemed stable and quiet, perhaps only

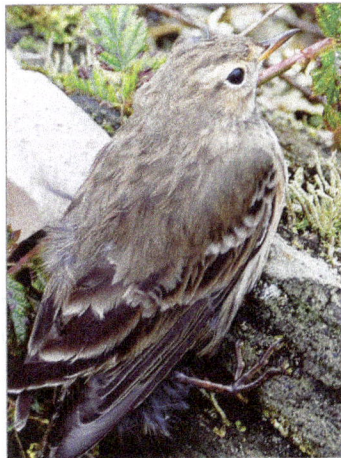

Songbird #10-452.

stunned and needing time to recover. I drove to a turnout up the way to evaluate its injuries.

Bird in hand, I walked to the edge of the prairie, swung my legs over a lichen-covered log, and sat down with my feet firmly planted in the grass looking out across Haro Strait. The wide-eyed bird watched me. And I watched it, and memorized a faint white eye ring, pale cream brow, thin two-toned bill, amber feet, and soft, streaky breast. I spoke to it with quiet reassurance. "Let's just relax here and see how you are doing," I said.

I was not sure what species my charge was: not a sparrow; not a lark; not a warbler. It was young. I could tell from the plumage, but what was its name? I took a photograph to jog my memory later.

After a few minutes, I placed the little traveler on a piece of drift beside the log. It held on gamely with tiny three-toed feet, stayed still, and glanced my way as if to say, "Now what?" The bird was alert. That was good. Then spontaneously, it leaped into the air and plummeted in a flurry of disarrayed feathers to the sandy substrate and toppled over. "Oh, no! Broken wing," I sighed. It peeped softly and regained its footing. I could see there was blood on the underside of the right wing and a spot of red at the left eye. The little bird needed help. I placed it back on the log beside me. It perched calmly and did not try again to fly. It seemed attentive to the surroundings.

From past experience, I knew the odds of a young bird's survival with a concussion and badly broken wing were not good. I felt a narrowing of its time between this world and the next and so, before leaving for the drive across the island to the Wolf Hollow Wildlife Center, I tarried some moments wanting to give the injured one a little longer in its realm. Clouds were breaking. The sun had come up in the east over Mt. Baker and was lighting the way to the prairie. There were cracks of blue in the dawn sky. Dew sparkled on silver spider webs in the tall, sweet-smelling grass; the cricket chorus was warming up. There was an ochre ringlet butterfly—often a fine meal for small birds—still roosting on spent nipplewort nearby. It was 50-some degrees—fine weather for flying. We both sat quietly and took in the air. Then, it was time to go.

No matter all of our best efforts, the beautiful little songbird could not be saved. Shona Aitken identified it as an immature American pipit. Ah, of course. I had not recognized it at first in unfinished plumage, but now it seemed clear. And, as a flocking bird, I had encountered the youngster with a dozen or so of its kin. It had been given an admission number at Wolf Hollow: Songbird #10-452, written on a piece of lavender note paper.

At midday, I drove back to American Camp with the pipit. I chose her final resting place on the east side of Cattle Point Road, just down from Pickett's Lane. I laid Pipit to rest in a deep depression of grasses and moss beside a glacial erratic with a view across Griffin Bay to Mt. Baker. It was as close as I could come to marking the southern most point of the pipit's migration journey. As I finished the task, I promised the bright shining bird with the golden eyes that her bad luck and untimely death would not go unnoticed. In some way, I would make sure her life mattered. And while she did not likely hear my words, somewhere in her soul I hoped Pipit understood.

Now, years later, I still have that piece of lavender note paper and my promise to Songbird #10-452. So, may I tell you about pipits?

~

Pipits take my breath away. They always have. The first time I saw them at American Camp many years ago, I didn't know what the scattered flock of little brown birds were—strutting about the grassland as if they owned it. The sun shone down on the robin-sized birds' streaky breasts turning the plumage from modest, buffy hues into a dazzling yellow sheen, the color of soft, finely churned butter. The songbirds flung themselves into the air to snatch butterflies from a split rail fence; ran—not hopped or fluttered—across the substrate, snaring grasshoppers, beetles and such; and used glacial erratics as perch sites to access their domain. What was that quirky two-note call they used when startled into the air only to come back down just a short distance away? Their dark eyes gleamed with intensity. I was hooked and, ever since, watch for the golden birds each early September as the pipits make their way south from northern breeding grounds, or possibly from nearby Cascadia alpine meadows.

Little brown birds, indeed. That they travel in loose flocks during migration only adds to their anonymity. The details of their lives largely go unnoticed by all but the most committed observers. Passersby at South Beach are not likely to ask where these birds are from—if they notice them at all, where they are going, or why it matters. It is all about perception, I suppose. That it matters to me is simply my truth—nothing more.

Now that I know them, I easily recognize the pipits from the savannah, vesper, song, and Lincoln's sparrows (among others) and larks that share this habitat. I like their crisp lines, jaunty gait, and high-strung ways. I am high-strung, too. It always energizes me to see them.

First, it is the vanguards I find in the early fall, the advanced team with their lofty calls. *Pi-pip, pip-it*, the birds shout, and thus their common name. As the days flow into mid-month, dozens or hundreds more appear. I see them on the grasslands at American Camp, the mudflats at False Bay, in pastures in San Juan Valley, perched on chain-linked fencing at the airport, or foraging along the bluffs on the west side—all open space habitats where they can glean the last warmth of the September sun as they head south.

In years gone by, I have seen thousands of pipits in a single day. One September at Cattle Point I wrote in my journal: "… pipits are pouring through the islands now. They are everywhere: in the grass, on the beaches, and noisily scurrying along the bluffs. The buff on their breasts and sides resembles the color of aged driftwood."

One of my favorite ornithologists and author of several volumes on the birds of Ohio, Washington State and California, William Leon Dawson called pipits "nomads." In 1909, he wrote: "As the flock comes straggling down from the north land, they utter unceasing yips of mild astonishment and self-reproach at their apparent inability to decide what to do next." Or, I might add, where to go.

Watching pipits during their stopover on San Juan revealed a lot about their nature. First, they are walkers rather than fly-ers when foraging. They have adapted a long hind toe (hallux) that helps them maneuver on uneven ground. One day at South Beach, I encountered a flock busily foraging while trending to-ward the south end of the island. I decided to walk a spell with them along the backbeach. This shoreline, a bit over two miles from the parking lot to Cattle Point, is layered laterally—a sandy beach just off Haro Strait, then a jumbled driftwood line edging a sand and gravelly tilled substrate of sedge, bracken, seasonal wildflowers and shrubs, then onto the grassy ridge that sweeps up into the dunes and, to the southeast, the terraced slope of Mt. Finlayson. I wrote about this realm in *Rainshadow World*. It is considered by most a barren, disheveled wasteland. Noth-ing could be farther from the truth. In the spring, the area is lush with seashore lupine, beach pea, seaside fiddleneck, silver bursage, yellow sand-verbena, beach morning glory and many more species of flowering plants. It is a butterfly haven and high-ly prized habitat for migrators each fall.

It was great fun walking with, watching, and listening to the spir-ited pipits making their living. They scurried southward along huge piles of drift mingled with beach grass and American sea rocket snatching bugs from every crevice while I dodged sand wasps on the trail. They bobbed their tails with exuberance—likely a good balancing strategy.

At one point, they diverted to the beach poking at three spirals of bull kelp that had rolled in on the tide and were rife with insects. Their competition for the feast were insect-eating western and least sandpipers, dunlins and black-bellied plovers among other shore-birds. Here, it was my turn to keep my balance on the drift. I peered over the huge logs as the pipits detoured to the water's edge.

Offshore, hundreds of surf scoters, red-breasted mergansers, and red-necked and horned grebes cruised the inland sea diving for small fish to satisfy their appetites. Seven Pacific loons were impressive with silvery napes. One common loon, still in breeding plumage, emitted its signature, haunting call that echoed along the shore. The cacophony of bird sounds was loud and thrilling. The pipits modest two-note call mingled with this sound track of migration.

Farther down the way, past a makeshift driftwood hut, the pipits nudged savannah sparrows out of their path with an uncharacteristic burst of noisy chatter. These summer residents were getting ready to head south, as well, garbed in streaky brown and tan plumes with defining yellow lores; they were a bit smaller than the pipits. Kill-deer, another saucy shorebird, voiced its own piercing admonition at the intrusion by the pipits. *Kil-dee, Kil-dee*, it shouted for all to hear. Killdeer are well known to me on this backbeach. Three months before, I had watched a female execute her broken-wing display to lure me away from her humble nest of stones, laying eggs bare on the glacial till.

I kept my distance from this loose flock of pipits. Every time I tried to get a closer look, the migrators started with a sharp *yip* and rose into the air only to alight a few yards down the strand. They didn't seem to be in a hurry. I wasn't either. The pace allowed me to look about at who else was joining the pipits on their epic journey or using this habitat other times of the year.

I walked carefully east past spent beach pea, knowing that just months before the western tailed blue butterflies had been active there. Now, the larvae of the next generation were sleeping securely in desiccated pea pods in the sand awaiting emergence next spring. Echo azures and silvery blues were there, also, and two highly endangered species: the island marble butterfly (overwintering as pupae) and the sand-verbena moth that overwinters as larvae deeply embedded in the sand. I learned long ago to be mindful of every step I take along the backbeach. What some may consider a wasteland, I understand to be a rich biological realm to navigate with care. Every footprint on the sand had meaning to the wildlife there.

~

Salmon Bank! Walking the backbeach often, I was mindful of the habitat's rich cultural history. This sandy substrate was once the spring and summer home to the Coast Salish who camped in mat houses or plank homes while reef netting and trolling for salmon, among other activities, at what is now known as Salmon Bank. They predated European settlement here by thousands of years. The shoreline and marine resources continue to hold significance to current Indigenous residents.

The Bank is a geologic formation—a submerged ridge located a mile off the southern shore of San Juan Island in the Strait of Juan de Fuca formed by the advance and retreat of glacial ice sheets tens of thousands of years ago. The relatively shallow water (ten fathoms deep in places) brings salmon that are heading, in hoards, for spawning grounds on the Fraser and other northern rivers. They swim close to the surface enabling enormous catches by fishers.

With the coming of Europeans, the nature of this shoreline enclave changed dramatically. Early settlers and explorers, looking for riches, dubbed the area "the best fishing grounds in Puget

Sound." Soon, the Hudson's Bay Company insinuated itself into the far-reaching, fish-rich economy. Improvements in the design of fish traps by non-natives and large commercial enterprises ensued. Massive amounts of fish were taken from the Bank and local economies boomed from the late 1880s to early 1900s. The major offshore fishing operations required onshore facilities to house workers and equipment. This backbeach and ridge was transformed into a tent village (The Salmon Bank Beach Camp) with numerous makeshift shacks, dormitories and a cook house allowing the workers close proximity to their lucrative operation. Once fish traps were banned, the economic boom subsided in the 1920s, the beach community disbanded, and this landscape reverted to its natural state.

~

Now, back in real time, I spied a flock of about thirty horned larks a little farther back from the drift line. They were doing their own scouting on the sand (likely for seeds rather than insects) with a different variation of the three-toed walk of the pipits. They had molted out of their breeding plumage into less conspicuous garb. Their feathers were gray above and white below, minus the ear tufts (horns) of the breeding season. Faint black bibs were their only sure identifiers—at least, for me. I could have missed even this sizable flock had I not been actively looking for them; their sandy plumes were that perfect along the substrate.

My first encounter with horned larks had been near Churchill, Manitoba some years before. I had joined a team of biologists on a study of beluga whales in the Churchill River. Shortly after my arrival, I did a walkabout the tundra near the Beluga Motel where we were staying. I saw a small flock of larks foraging in the sand. It was July. They were in full breeding plumage, their "horns"—actually tufts of dark, horn-like feathers on each side of the crown—were highly visible. I stopped and took photographs. They seemed uncon-cerned by my presence. I was thrilled to see them. I continued my exploration. It was only when I returned an hour later to the deck of the motel that my friend Jim Short suggested I turn around and look back at the landscape. I did. I spied a fine, young polar bear coming our way. It had been following me and likely contemplating its op-tions—and mine. Needless to say, I did not venture out alone, again.

Back at American Camp—not a polar bear in sight—these horned larks were also intent on foraging and seemed more earnest than the pipits, staying in a tighter formation and determined to make head-way south. "Are you going to walk all the way to Mexico instead of flying?" I queried them with a smile. The breeze ruffled their feathers—and my hair—and we walked on toward the lighthouse. Their pace was quicker than mine, though, and soon they were out of sight and only their tracks remained in the sand.

I am often reminded—watching flocking birds—that each individ-ual has its own story separate from the other members of the group. Here on the backbeach, over time, I had watched flocks of immature and adult horned larks—each going their separate ways after fledg-ing. Had the immatures merged and mingled with other young larks from different locations, I wondered, having come together with a common goal—making their first journey south to their wintering rounds safely within the security of the flock? Some would make it and some would not. I knew that. And, thus, more reason to admire them here in their beautiful and unique forms and ways.

I rejoined the pipits and walked a bit farther with them toward Cattle Point. Occasionally, I saw them doubling back over former ground looking like they were not quite sure where they were going. I was reminded of Dawson's quote from the northland about the pipits wondering what to do next. I concluded there was actually a fine-tuned motivation in their momentary disarray. They knew exactly what they were doing.

Soon, it was time for a break. As I sat along the shore, I saw some of the pipits were resting as well—seeking shade in the crevices and overhangs of the drift. Elsewhere in the park, I noticed they rested and sought security in the shade of split rail fencing. More often, though, they disappeared into the tall grass where they roosted at night, perhaps not far from the newly arrived western meadowlarks who would be spending the winter here.

The tide was coming in. It was still a far piece to the lighthouse. I wondered if the tidal surge over the rocky outcrops ahead might block my way, so I decided to leave the pipits for a spell and rejoin them later at Cattle Point Lighthouse. Soon enough, we reconnected. This rocky shoreline was a bit different habitat than the back-beach to the north. Ever the nimble, opportunistic foragers, the pipits wasted no time exploiting the outcrops gleaning insects and worms from the crusty substrate. They widely dispersed, moving constantly, energized perhaps by the surf. They bobbed their heads pigeon-like, and their tails up and down, and fluttering from rock to rock. Walking did not work here.

I was surprised how close they got to the spray zone barely escaping the waves on several occasions. I saw one adult taking a bath in a tidepool, letting the water spill over its feet and dunking in the saltwater. That seemed brave, but I knew the behavior had been minutely calibrated by the pipit to stay safe.

They rounded the point below the lighthouse. A group of black oystercatchers did not like being displaced and called out their displeasure with searing chants. Two pipits flew toward the sandy beach by the Compass House seeking the last rays of the sun, I supposed. The others continued to mingle along the shore.

It was time for me to go. I headed back to my car along the bluff trail flushing nearly a dozen pipits who were resting in the grass. I knew they would settle down again up the way. I had thoroughly enjoyed my walkabout with the pipits down South

Beach—a glimpse into their lives I would always value. The little brown birds had a long journey ahead. They would not be walking all the way. I thanked them for their time and wished them well. "Safe travels, little pipits."

And now, months later, writing this story, I wonder about the size of the pipit's universe, and where those beautiful birds are sleeping tonight.

12

SEEKER OF WANDERING STONES

A northern shrike arrived on the island for the winter. America's only predatory songbird's unflattering reputation preceded it, but what was the real truth behind its elegant silver sheen?

A streak of silver shot down from a red elderberry bush beyond a split rail fence on Redoubt Road. A dapper gray bird snatched a grasshopper from the dusty way, flew to a blackberry bush, impaled the insect on the thorny barbs of the vine and used its small, shiny black feet to hold the hopper in place while it fed.

The bird was a northern shrike—America's only predatory songbird—newly arrived from its summer in the open spaces of boreal forests along the taiga/tundra boundary of Canada and Alaska. I had witnessed the signature characteristic of this efficient bird: spiking its prey in a manner that had led to its scurrilous reputation as a heartless evildoer and killer of harmless quarry.

Not all birds are beloved. Especially in the early days of ornithology, some species' predatory behavior led to their being rebuked as evil or wicked—often maligned in colorful language in old texts that have sadly stood the test of time. Even today, these birds may be regarded less for beauty than for perceived cruelty in the manners they employ while making a living in a perilous world. I have watched such a bird on San Juan Island and, rejecting its bad press, followed its winter residency here with deep appreciation for its beauty and unorthodox ways.

It was a perfect afternoon for naturing. The air was dry and still on one of the last warm days of summer before the rains came. At American Camp, hundreds of acres of grassland glowed gold in the late afternoon sun. The sky was a perfect cornflower blue, reminiscent of still-blooming chicory growing along the way. The cold, blue-green water of Haro Strait shimmered off South Beach as I walked along the scruffy plain looking for migrating birds and butterflies. I could hear the whistling wingbeats of surf scoters taking off from over the ridge—east—at Griffin Bay. The bees were still faintly buzzing in the papery white blooms of a favored patch of pearly everlasting, and the grasshoppers, while nearly gone, chirped a forlorn farewell to summer. Mostly, though, there was gilded silence in the grass.

As I turned onto Redoubt Road, I saw the shrike. It perched unassuming on the branch of that elderberry amidst clusters of lance-shaped leaves and ripened fruit: robin-sized with a palette of blue-gray plumage above, long black tail with white outer tail feathers, and black wings with white wing patches. Its most striking physical feature was a dark line—resembling a mask—running behind and through the eyes to a strong hooked beak. These shades of gray, black and white were perfect camouflage on the monotone landscape of the shrike's wintering grounds. This bird looked a bit brownish, though, and I wondered if it might be in its first year. I took a photo to ponder later.

The shrike was perch hunting from boulders, split rails, and small trees and shrubs along the road. It repeated the behavior of retrieving and impaling grasshoppers several times as I watched from the shade of an old crab apple tree.

Shrikes are migratory birds that herald the transition from summer to fall in the Pacific Northwest. Long ago, they were called butcher bird, nine killer and winter butcher by biologists and birders. It was reviled for its relentless hunting prowess often taking small birds equal to its own size. Shrike has a propensity for hanging prey upside down much as a butcher might hang meat in a locker—thus the moniker. Far from being the eccentricity of a small, gray bird, the strategy is a way to cache food for future use in lean times, or for the birds to mark their territories. The predator lacks talons and thus dispatches prey by forcing it to the ground, then using its strong hooked bill to kill with a series of bites to the neck. Shrike has adapted the behavior of skewering its victims on thorns or lodging them in the crook of tree branches so it can gain leverage while it feeds.

Shrike's common name appears to have come from the Old English word "scric" meaning shriek, referring to its shrill, piercing call.

Neltje Blanchan, author of *Bird Neighbors* first published in 1897, wrote about the shrike: "Not even a hawk itself can produce the consternation among a flock of sparrows that the harsh, rasping voice of the butcher bird creates, for escape they well know to be difficult before the small ogre swoops down upon his victim, and carries it off to impale it on a thorn or frozen twig, there to devour it later piecemeal. Every shrike thus either impales or else hangs up, as a butcher does his meat, more little birds of many kinds ... than it can hope to devour in a week of bloody orgies."

Naturalist and nature writer John Burroughs declared his disgust for Shrike in *Locusts and Wild Honey* (1886) characterizing the bird as an assassin, wolf in sheep's clothing, Bluebeard and butcher among other disparagements.

Ornithologist William Dawson added this in 1909: "All times are killing time for this bloodthirsty fellow, and even in winter he "jerks" the meat not necessary for present consumption—be it chilly-footed mouse or palpitating Sparrow—upon some convenient thorn or splinter."

The supposed evildoer returned to San Juan Island right on schedule. It arrived in clear, calm skies that would soon turn sullen, wet, and wind-blown.

Shrike is a creature of habit. Many birds—and other animals—have what biologists call site fidelity. They show a high degree of reliability in their movements about and between breeding grounds and overwintering habitats. They may return to the location of their birth, to a familiar winter retreat, a staging area prior to migration, a food-rich stopover during migration, or even a traditionally safe place to molt.

Think for a moment how in the early spring you may see a hummingbird levitate in front of your kitchen window as if to announce its return and encourage you to put a feeder back out on the porch. Is it the same bird that visited you the year before? There is evidence to support that possibility, and don't we wish it to be true?

I counted on site fidelity to find shrikes each fall. It often took only a few minutes scanning a familiar open habitat to spot the handsome bird perched atop an elderberry, hawthorn, blackberry vine, or a signpost. Any vantage point would do. This year was no exception.

I downloaded my photograph of Shrike from that first encounter and enlarged the image. I could make out pencil-thin ripples of gray barring across its creamy breast and, as I suspected, a brownish mask that was not yet fully formed. These details suggested it might be an immature bird, on its own for the first time on this wintering ground. Was it kin to the adult shrike I saw in this spot last year, or had this youngster simply been first to claim its niche in this ideal habitat?

I stopped along the road often through November to check on Shrike. Far from being a bloodthirsty villain, I found it a calm presence on the plain possessing a solitary watchfulness that appealed to me for it is in solitude that I observed it and felt most at home.

The masked bird with the silver sheen was always quiet—scanning the plains with keen, dark eyes. When the raucous gang of resident crows flew by, as they often did, Shrike retained its tranquil mind. The mischievous corvids could not break its concentration.

Shrike was ever mindful, though, of the nearest cover whether into the grass or sometimes to the same crab apple tree I had used earlier as shade. It usually held its hunting ground against intrusion but one afternoon I noticed Shrike disappeared, and the meadowlarks suddenly ceased their ebullient songs. Moments later, a sleek peregrine falcon, top predator of this realm, flashed past me and careened over the ridge. I was glad Shrike had good survival skills.

~

Shrike continued its bounding from boulder to fence line to shrubby perches throughout the fall. It appeared to like best the lofty vantage point of big boulders. The rocks seemed possessed with an air of entitlement to this plain. The massive stones had come here long before Shrike, bearing witness to the eras-old geologic past of this place.

The boulders were glacial erratics—products of the Pleistocene Ice Age that began tens of thousands of years ago. The name was derived from the Latin "errare" meaning to wander. Long past, massive sheets of glacial ice advanced through the archipelago and south over what we now call the Puget Lowlands, then retreated into British Columbia's Coastal Mountains. The warming of those frozen rivers left enormous rocks and smaller stones behind as they fell out of the melting flows.

Glacial erratic at American Camp.

One day, waiting for Shrike, I strolled the once ice-bound barrens carefully sidestepping rabbit warrens while admiring the lush winter coat of the red fox waiting nearby for me to move on. Fifty yards west—toward the sea—I could make out two dozen black-bellied plovers gleaning in the grass and pebble-strewn substrate. Their halting gait and short scurries were unmistakable. There were dunlins, too, much smaller shorebirds travelling with the flock. Every tuft of grass and mound of dirt had meaning to these nomads—returning every fall to this exact spot to fill those black bellies—now winter white—before moving on.

The erratics—defined as stones different in size and type from local bedrock—were a conspicuous presence on this lateral landscape. The wandering stones were beautifully scattered about with intriguing informality varying in magnitude from palm-sized rocks and pebbles to massive boulders weighing several tons. The stones differed in color, too, from black to gray to white: solid, speckled, finely veined and often pockmarked from their eons of weathering. There were scars and scrapes, as well, from their long journeys of sometimes hundreds of miles along the coastline of Cascadia. I picked up one of the stones. It fit perfectly in the palm of my hand. I ran my fingers over its smooth, buffy surface: oval, almost pyriform, with small black speckles and blotches. I wondered where it was from and how long it took to make the journey south to this place. Each stone had its own story to tell. But there was more. Pondering the stone, I realized it was a near replica (if larger) of a killdeer's egg—another shorebird of this place. I knew Killdeer well and often watched it scurry among the plovers. Killdeer was a permanent resident; each spring she laid four tiny, speckled eggs in a nest of stones and shells on this bare substrate. The resemblance was startling. Those eggs hide in plain sight among the glacial till.

The best-known glacial erratic at American Camp is Robert's Rock at The Redoubt. This huge hunchbacked boulder, nearly ten feet high by seven paces, is a cornerstone of the nearly 700-square-foot earthen fortification designed during the Pig War to protect the camp from British insurgence. The stronghold was never tested in the twelve-year joint occupation. The only shot fired killed a British pig. Redoubt engineer Lt. Henry Robert moved on from his San Juan Island post to a long military career and was perhaps better known for developing *Robert's Rules of Order.*

$\sim$

Those rules still stand, as does the stone bearing Robert's name. A close examination of the fractured granite revealed gouges, grooves and striations from the pressure of the ancient ice flows. Robert's Rock and other erratics were splashed with intricately patterned gray-green, orange and black lichens some resembling sunbursts, states and, there was the boot of Italy. Dense fluorescent green mosses nourished other organisms. Looking closer, I could see tiny insects maneuvering in the moss and realized these erratics were acting as mini-ecosystems on a prairie landscape where all things are connected.

The boulders were not just sitting there, so to speak. There was life flowing from them as they served many functions for wildlife. The northern shrike wasn't the only bird that perch hunted from these pioneers. Kestrels, merlins, short-eared owls, and northern flickers appreciated the vantage point; songbirds like robins and savannah sparrows used these lofty thrones to shout their springtime songs across the prairie attracting mates and claiming territory. I have watched both mountain bluebirds and western bluebirds surveying the plains from these perches during their migrations through and summer residencies here. Butterflies and dragonflies basked on the warm rocks in summer, garter snakes and lizards sought the shade of their rough-edged pedestals, and soil produced by continuing erosion

157

trapped seeds and nourished native wildflowers and grasses including camas, chocolate lilies and fescue. In *Rainshadow World*, I wrote
about a gathering of ladybug beetles overwintering in the crevice of
a glacial erratic entwined with elderberry. They can be rich habitats.

There were rock piles, too, scattered about the American Camp
landscape. They reflected the early human history of the park. Indigenous people cultivated camas here thousands of years ago throwing
small erratics aside to clear and fire their patches. The Hudson's
Bay Company's presence beginning in the early 1850s meant that
wandering rocks were cast aside for cart paths or formed fences or
building foundations. The military occupation during the Pig War
accelerated the clearing, but it was when early European settlers
homesteaded the land following the war that the greatest impacts
were felt upon the land. Large areas were cleared and plowed for
agriculture and sheep pastures. The stacked rocks were often sited
next to large erratics that were too heavy to move. Those cairns—
easily visible from roads and trails—exist now as historic markers
and reminders of our past, but significant to present-day wildlife
still making a living on the plain.

Shrike used the rock piles, too. And, it hunted at the Parade
Grounds where in the 1860s an entire community of soldiers lived
and worked. It swooped downslope past the restored Laundry
Quarters and across Home Prairie—the Hudson's Bay Company's
once bustling Belle Vue Sheep Farm—and down to Alaska Packer
Rock and the freshwater spring. Robert's Rock remains the perfect
perch for Shrike to oversee this domain.

Another favored perch for Shrike was a tattered elderberry that
grew out of an erratic next to an old rectangular basin measuring
nearly four feet by twenty-two feet at the south end of the road. I
asked local historian Boyd Pratt what it was and he suggested—because of its cement base and sloped entry at one end—likely a sheep
dip trough used by ranchers after the turn into the 20th century.

The surrounding rocks may have defined the remnants of a holding area for the sheep before being dipped. The present Redoubt Road was originally a sheep run to the station or a trail to Old Town Lagoon build by Hudson's Bay Company employees and Cowichan native laborers.

Historians Mike & Julia Vouri's book *San Juan Island* includes a photograph from 1908, which shows the road. Vouri comments: "The county road, bordered by a split rail fence, follows pretty much the same route as the Redoubt Road in San Juan Island National Historical Park, only then it terminated near today's Jakle's Lagoon trailhead."

The sheep dip station—now a seeming haphazard jumble of rocks—was a little piece of history about this land nearly lost but drawn attention to by Shrike.

⁓

Time passed on Redoubt Road. Shrike remained patient with my continuing appearances along the way. It was graceful and concise in its swift, fluttering flight over the grass, and agile enough to pick insects out of the air while still stationed at its favorite perches.

Early fall turned into a cold, blustery December. Still, I stopped by to check on Shrike. One such day, a storm was brewing over Haro Strait out of the North Pacific. The Witness Tree—a venerable old Douglas fir that had stood along this way for generations—watched me arrive. The ancient conifer was scarred by fire, pockmarked by woodpeckers, girdled by an ax, and broken topped and its branches swept to the east by the wind. Yet, it remained undaunted and invaluable to wildlife there. Over the years, I had counted over two dozen species of birds, mammals, butterflies and dragonflies that used the Witness Tree as part of their life experience. It remained an especially good perch for the peregrine falcon, robins and northern flickers in winter, and bald eagles and returning hummingbirds in the spring. I stopped, as I always did, to pay my respects to the old-timer and smiled at recalling on my last visit here western meadowlarks had been nearby—a small flock of about a dozen—dozing in the tall grass. Just before I moved on, a small chorus of liquid notes bubbled out of the grass into the crisp fall air.

I like best William Dawson's recollection of listening to meadowlarks. He wrote: "… on a nippy October morning … there comes a sound which brings us to our feet. We hasten to the window, throw up the sash and lean out into the cool, fresh air while a Meadowlark rehearses, all at a sitting, the melodies of the year's youth. It all comes back to us with a rush; the smell of lush grasses; the splendor of apple blossoms, the courage of lengthening days, the exstacies (sic) of courtship—all these are recalled by the lark-song. It is as though this fore-thoughtful soul had caught the music of a May day, just at its prime, in a crystal vase, and was now pouring out the imprisoned sound in a gurgling, golden flood …"

And now, how sweet this song retold again and again by the old field lark on our island prairie for all brave souls to hear in the shadow of the Witness Tree and bluster of a coming storm.

I found Shrike, as usual, at the sheep dip station perched on the elderberry at the trough. The tempo of the wind had changed—kicking up hard. Tufts of creamy reindeer lichen torn from their holdfasts in the sand were hurtling across the substrate like tumbleweeds. The incoming cloud bank took on the texture of soot. The air was getting almost too cold to breathe so I watched Shrike from my car.

The agile bird kept its balance in the growing gale by pumping its long black tail and holding on to the elderberry with those strong black feet. Through my binoculars I could see the gray plumage on its back was the color of the gathering cumulus clouds. All the other shades of gray of this December moment were perfect camouflage for the Watcher Bird of old: the gray bark on the elderberry, the erratics in the yard, the pebbles on the road, aging split rails, and the prairie grass worn and faded after a long, hot summer.

A flock of crows careened by on an especially strong gust of westward wind further energizing the air. Sometimes, the black birds touched down for a short exuberant dance in the stone rectangle—especially at twilight, but it was too blustery today.

A battered black pickup truck sped by next to the elderberry loudly bouncing through the pot holes on the road and kicking up dust. Shrike flushed and flew low with three wingbeats and an undulating glide to the thicket at the junction to Pickett's Lane. It perched atop ocean spray but didn't stay long. Appearing impatient in the restless wind, the agile hunter tried leaning into it and soon flung itself off the branch and hovered over the grass. I counted the beats: one, two, three seconds and on to fifteen when it took a sharp dive into the grassy maze likely having spotted a mouse or vole. No luck. Back to its perch. A second dive and then away.

Shrike would not go far, of that, I was sure. This landscape of wind and wandering rocks was its winter home—its hunting ground—as with the peoples of the past. The once butcher bird had unwittingly—through its movements about the landscape—encouraged my curiosity about the geologic and human history for this place. Each epoch here changed the landscape into a different story. At the moment, Shrike was directing the narrative—helping keep the spirit of the land alive. Far from being an evildoer, I found the beautiful bird an excellent guide to the mysteries of this gray plain.

One prairie. One Shrike. One life. The land was changing almost before our eyes, yet somehow remained the same. Both of us were connected to this place along the Salish Sea and to one another. Separate yet inseparable. I was eager to see where Shrike would lead me next.

13
WHO VISITS
THE WITNESS TREE?

*The grand old Douglas fir stands alone
along Redoubt Road bearing witness
to changing times on the prairie.*

Estimated at over one hundred years old, the Witness Tree has nurtured wildlife, withstood the onslaught of Pacific gales, and evoked admiration from passers-by.

Broken by wind, chiseled by woodpeckers, scarred by fire, and gnarled by time. Its deeply furrowed trunk is laden with lichens, mosses and memories of times past.

The old-timer sometimes holds precious nests. It is a perfect perch for eagles, peregrine falcons, hawks, meadowlarks and a multitude of smaller birds. Robins greet the day atop its canopy and white-crowned sparrows sing their spring songs from its boughs. Delicate chartreuse cones unfurl each spring with the promise of generations to come.

The Witness Tree sees all. Throughout our lifetimes, it remains an indomitable presence on the prairie and an old and treasured friend to us all.

Northern Saw-Whet Owl.

Witness Tree Visitors

- [ ] California Quail
- [ ] Anna's Hummingbird
- [ ] Rufous Hummingbird
- [ ] Northern Harrier
- [ ] Bald Eagle
- [ ] Red-tailed Hawk
- [ ] Rough-legged Hawk
- [ ] Barred Owl
- [ ] Great Horned Owl
- [ ] Northern Saw-whet Owl
- [ ] Downy Woodpecker
- [ ] Hairy Woodpecker
- [ ] Northern Flicker
- [ ] Pileated Woodpecker
- [ ] American Kestrel
- [ ] Merlin
- [ ] Peregrine Falcon

- [ ] Northern Shrike
- [ ] Northwest Crow
- [ ] Common Raven
- [ ] Violet-green Swallow
- [ ] No. Rough-winged Swallow
- [ ] Barn Swallow
- [ ] Chestnut-backed Chickadee
- [ ] Red-breasted Nuthatch
- [ ] American Robin
- [ ] European Starling
- [ ] American Goldfinch
- [ ] Fox Sparrow
- [ ] Dark-eyed Junco
- [ ] White-crowned Sparrow
- [ ] Golden-crowned Sparrow
- [ ] Western Meadowlark

14

BLUEBIRDS
IN THE RAIN

*This western bluebird looked out
over San Juan Valley from its perch
at Red Mill Farm. The native blues
are home again after an over
fifty-year absence.*

The gathering gray clouds of late fall held the island in their grasp. Sitting still outside wasn't as easy, or comfortable, as it had been in the captivating months of sunshine, birdsongs and blooming wildflowers. Yet, an unexpected event cheered me toward the shortest day of the year.

On December 3, I drove to Lime Kiln. It was time for large flocks of American robins to forage on the lush berries of Pacific madrones—massive contorted-framed trees that were so important to wildlife in the park. Hundreds of the "red breasts" gathered in late fall and winter amidst the shiny, evergreen leaves of *Arbutus menziesii*. The cacophonous calls and wild wingbeats of the frenzied feeders resonated winter's exuberant but often overlooked energy.

Temperatures were in the forties. A kick of south wind rattled the leaves in the trees at Westside Preserve as I arrived. There were still lots of intact berries—beautiful orange orbs that glistened in the low light—but no robins. A disappointment.

Then, at high noon, in a big-leaf maple along the rocky bluff by the deep-green inland sea, a flash of blue. Then another. Six western bluebirds were skittering through the maples and along the grassy slope chattering softly to one another. In the frail light, I could define at least three males in the group; the blue on their wings easily identifying the birds. The "blues" were calm and intent on foraging. I stayed in the car and watched, not wanting to disturb them. After twenty minutes, I drove around the corner to Deadman's Bay to check the maples there. No bluebirds, but lots of wind. It picked up sharply. By the time I got back to the Preserve the blues had moved on—or taken cover.

I texted Kathleen Foley at the San Juan Preservation Trust. She had been working tirelessly on a program reintroducing western bluebirds to San Juan Island and been extremely successful. K. had been out on the west side the day before looking for the bluebirds, but was rebuffed by the wind. I gave her the great sighting news and she texted back: "Hooray!" This was the first sighting of overwintering western bluebirds on the island in the current era—a big deal and joyous occasion.

Months before the auspicious December sighting, I had visited The Trust's field station across the island and had my first close encounters with the iconic western bluebirds. That event gave me insight into the blues' place in island natural history. The birds made an indelible impression on me well worth recounting here.

On August 1, the sun rose over San Juan Valley in a watercolor-washed sky of powder blue, brushed with strands of creamy pearl. There was a hint of a blue moon hanging high among the cirrus clouds as I arrived at Red Mill Farm.

There was an aura about the picturesque farm set among ancient Garry oaks on a rise overlooking the valley, False Bay and the Strait of Juan de Fuca beyond. From sheep ranch to dairy farm and, since the 1960s, pasture land and residence of beloved islanders Ernie and

Dodie Gann, Red Mill seemed to have been settled upon rarified air. It would be an understatement to say we feel a deep sense of gratitude to the Ganns for their decades of commitment to land conservation and the ultimate bequest of perpetual protection of 760-acres of cherished landscape. It seemed fitting that the bluebirds should call Red Mill Farm home.

The Ganns coveted their privacy after decades of high adventure and achievement around the world. They purchased one hundred acres in San Juan Valley in 1965 and continued to add to the property over the years. It was the perfect place for Ernie to continue writing and, in later years, to concentrate on his painting. He remarked to a reporter in 1991 of his good fortune: "Not even a Russian grand duke had anything like this. There is nothing like this in the world, where you can ride from valley to the sea or to the mountain—all of nature is right here."

Years later, Dodie—by now an avid land preservationist—added: "It you have something like this, you don't want to lose it. It's a wonderful thing to save it forever." This remarkable couple did just that.

~

The hedgerows of Nootka rose, snowberry and wild blackberry bustled with butterflies as I headed up the driveway to the converted field station. A family of California quail scurried through the underbrush, towhees and wrens scattered, and a flock of goldfinch—one of Dodie's favorite birds—cheerfully foraged in the thistle. There were dozens of Garry oak trees among the Douglas firs, Pacific madrones, big-leaf maples, and red alders gathered on mossy outcrops and grassy bald that adjoined the fertile fields. Collared doves cooed from their high perches in the old trees. Swallows swooped noisily overhead. Yellow-faced bumble bees busied themselves in grasses awash with Queen Anne's Lace. Golden dragonflies darted back and forth across the road as I passed the small orchard of apple and pear trees riddled with red-breasted sapsucker holes. The scene was set for my visit with the bluebirds.

Western bluebirds had become the symbol for the conservation of rapidly disappearing open savannah and Garry oak habitat in western Washington and elsewhere. Garry oaks (*Quercus garryana*) are invaluable wildlife trees. Their massive frames provide shade, cover, cavities (used as nest sites) for western bluebirds, kestrels and chickadees; and understory vegetation for ground-nesting birds like white-crowned sparrows and spotted towhees. The trees provide food in the form of acorns for band-tailed pigeons, and food in the form of insects, larvae and spiders for breeding birds and their offspring.

The decline of the oaks is not fully understood. There are poor records of their original abundance on the island according to the Land Bank's Doug McCutchen. Among the factors that contributed to their early demise were clearing for homesteads and agricultural use, loss of burning as part of ecosystem management, loss of predators that increased deer populations and browse, encroachment of Douglas fir forests, and competition with introduced plant and animal species. We may never know for sure if San Juan Valley was predominantly oak or a mosaic of shrubby wetland, oak associated wetland and patches of forest on the margins, as Doug suspects. He recalled an old map and description he found while researching the property that named the area "Oak Valley." That moniker evokes a splendid historical image of the scene.

Western bluebirds were once common residents in and migrants through the San Juan Islands. Like many songbirds, they fell prey to habitat loss. As the oak prairies diminished, the blues that historically used excavated woodpecker holes in the massive trees for nest sites declined, too. By the mid-20th century, they also fell victim to the vast invasion of European starlings that robbed them of nesting sites. While the blues do not appear to have been present during the

Pig War era, a survey taken in the 1930s noted them as common summer residents on the south slopes of Mount Dallas. According to Lewis and Sharpe's classic book *Birding in the San Juan Islands*: "… flocks of these birds were seen migrating on the south and west sides of San Juan in the fall and spring until 1963. The last reported breeding pair was present on Lopez in 1964."

Fifty years was a long time for the islands to be without the beautiful thrush. In 2007, The Preservation Trust partnered with several organizations in what started out as a five-year project to reestablish western bluebirds as a self-sustaining population and integral part of the island ecosystem. Now, nearly two decades later, the program is solidly established. Those wild, blue wings of summer are a familiar sight on parts of San Juan Island again.

~

Kathleen Foley Lewis was a beam of light—a force of nature in her dedication to protecting the bluebirds. The Conservation Project Manager for The Trust met me early at Red Mill for a status report. She bounded into the big room at the main house—the former Gann residence—with a welcoming smile that set off her fiery, long red hair pulled back into a no-nonsense braid to efficiently accommodate the busy day ahead. Her small frame packed a lot of energy. She was, as always, in perpetual motion, having just returned from the far side of the valley where she had checked on newly arrived breeding pairs of bluebirds brought in from Fort Lewis (JBLM) down Puget Sound on the mainland. We chatted a spell about the ups and downs of the program, then she was off again on more bluebird business. I would be on my own at Red Mill for the morning to get acquainted with a pair of blues using a nest box over by the orchard.

I settled into the gentle natural rhythm of the day by two large

Garry oaks that shaded the former Gann residence. I would sit still and let the bluebirds come my way to avoid any possibility of disturbing their routine. The oaks (*Quercus garryana*) were magnificent. The stout, heavy-bodied trees were a labyrinth of dense, gnarly branches laden with mosses, lichens, and fungi that support a vast matrix of life. Shadows from the deep green and celery splashed leaves played on the disheveled turf under the trees. They had aged gracefully and continued to thrive, producing healthy crops of acorns each summer. Subtle red flags marked several spots beneath the trees where oak seedlings have broken ground later to be transplanted elsewhere on the property.

It was quiet. There was a lot to take in as I waited for the blues to appear. With breeding season over for most birds, the jubilant warbling songs of spring had given way to the gentle strains of occasional hushed call notes emanating from high in the canopy. The silence was broken only by the sound of soft breezes from False Bay clattering through the leaves of the oaks, alders and poplars. It was hard to imagine that eons ago this valley had been literally underwater—assimilated into the inland sea when the sheets of glacial ice that had covered the island during the Fraser Glaciation melted. The accompanying rise in sea level inundated the landscape and, later receding, left the soil rich with marine nutrients.

I scanned the yard for bluebirds noting a feeding station set up near the Salish Seeds Nursery. Field techs left mealworms at the platform to supplement the diets of hungry adults and fledglings. Almost immediately, I saw a flash of bright blue wings levitating out of the tall grass in front of the caretaker's cottage. It was a male bluebird flushing insects from the sun-parched substrate. He dipped into the grass three times, appeared to almost nuzzle the ground, then came up with a mouth full of insects and headed toward the orchard. I knew there was an active nest box just behind an old pear tree and sure enough the male flew directly to the box on the split rail fence and disappeared into the cavity. Moments later, he reemerged and flew off along the perimeter lined with more nest boxes.

Soon, a juvenile bluebird brushed past me at the oak tree and landed on a post by the barn. Another followed close behind. These were, I assumed, the fledged offspring of the returning pair of wild blues I had heard about from Kathleen. The juveniles were active— flitting in short bursts from post to split rail to high atop a nearby apple tree and into the canopied layers of the oaks. They routinely checked the feeder waiting for the tech to arrive with mealworms. Their parents were busy with what was hoped would be a second brood of chicks.

Bluebirds are extravagantly colorful creatures, yet these juveniles' plumage was subtle and unfinished: soft brownish- gray with white-spotted breasts and backs, and hints of a rufous wash on the sides and breast and blue on the wings and tail. The fine lines would fill in soon enough on the males with bold ultramarine. For now, being understated was perhaps good camouflage for young birds not yet wise to the dangers of their new, wild world.

While watching the juveniles, I heard a soft tapping on the far side of an oak. It was a young hairy woodpecker working the deeply-furled trunk of the old tree. It used its fine long bill to pry moss and yellow lichens aside to get to good grubs in the deep folds of the tree. This young bird's plumage was not yet fully defined, either, and the soft gray lines on its back blended perfectly with the aging gray tree bark. Its presence here was a good example of oak habitat cohabitation. Hairy woodpeckers are cavity nesters and sometimes drill in the oaks—the excavations later used as nest sites by smaller breeding songbirds.

Sunlight playing through the leaves was soft and scintillating. A brown creeper foraged in another oak spiraling up and down the trunk gleaning with its downturned bill; a chestnut-backed chickadee made a quick pass through the canopy and was gone. Red-breasted nuthatches were there, too. I spied a cedar waxwing poking through the acorns. It glowed in shades of mustard and cinnamon brown and peered at me through dark eyes hidden behind its black mask. Band-tailed pigeons made a brief appearance nearby and, come fall, would return to take their fill of ripened acorns. All were important members of this oak habitat community.

Next to the waxwing, an adult bluebird perched quietly among the clusters of deeply lobed oak leaves taking in the valley view. I had not seen it arrive. The tranquil thrush did not stir as I walked under the tree to get a better vantage point. Such serenity. Through my binoculars, I could appreciate the subtle brilliance of its plumage: blue as the sky above, and "… the hue of the earth on its breast …" as naturalist John Burroughs wrote in 1871. Within moments I spied a second bluebird resting in the safe-haven oak.

It was a training day for the blues. The juveniles were learning and practicing new skills: how to perch hunt from the madrones and alders, to hover over tall grass in ground forage, and to work the oaks picking bugs from the leaves and cracks in the bark. They took cues from an adult male in finding secure vantage points. The fruit trees were favorites. Meantime, the breeding pair took turns delivering grubs to the nest box. They rarely made a sound except for subtle call notes. Their presence was statement enough.

There was only one moment of drama. A ruckus broke out in the sky as barn swallows mobbed an incoming merlin—a small, dark gray falcon well known for its hunting prowess. The air was a riot of wild alarm calls and the adult male bluebird perched atop a pear tree immediately dove for cover. The lives of these songbirds are fraught with danger. Even the relative safety of Red Mill Farm may not protect them from the myriad natural threats of this wild world.

At ten-thirty, biologist Kelsey Green appeared. She worked

with both The Trust and the Ecostudies Institute. Kelsey was responsible for daily monitoring of the bluebirds, and for transporting the families from JBLM (Joint Base Lewis/McChord) to the island that spring. I joined her to check the nest box. We waited for the female to leave, then Kelsey set a ladder up to take a look. She peered into the small wooden structure and, with a broad smile, announced the presence of four baby bluebirds that recently hatched. I took a quick look. Oh my, a bundle of naked nestlings in a woven grass womb. Their wide yellow mouths gapped open for food. Tiny strands of thin feathery dark-gray down adorned their crowns and backs. They looked a bit like little punk rockers. Bluebirds hatched under a blue moon. Perfect.

Satisfied that all was well, Kelsey put out mealworms for the adults who would be busy with the new brood. The juveniles could also use the added nutrition. Then, she prepared to head to another bluebird site to check on more nestlings. I was eager to join her for the next stop in her busy bluebird day.

Before we left, a brilliant male bluebird did a slow drift past me toward the tall grass near the split rail fence; its bright blue wings were wide open to the gentle breeze. An occasional, effortless beat kept the glide going. The scintillating bluebird seemed to float upon the grace of Red Mill Farm's enduring legacy to wildlife.

I joined Kelsey at another bluebird location in a grove of old oaks along Cattle Point Road. Close to a dozen juvenile and adult bluebirds foraged in the trees. Kelsey checked on more hatchlings at one of the nest boxes nearby. She removed two of the birds to check the progress of their emerging feathers, still encased in blue sheathes, then carefully returned them to the box. The nestlings were about eleven days old, and growing fast. Soon it would be time to band them before they fledged. The season was progressing well.

I rejoined Kelsey and Kathleen five days later to band the young birds. It was a cool, gray morning. After many years with bluebirds, Kathleen was a pro at the process. Four birds were carefully removed from the nest box and quickly given their color-coded leg bands. Kathleen gently cupped each tiny charge in her hands to ensure they did not get chilled in the moist air. While a simple process, it was still serious business; each move was carefully orchestrated to minimize stress on the birds. Kathleen had the touch. One baby blue fell asleep in her hand as the band was easily attached. In a few short days, these birds would be foraging about the oak grove and possibly moving into other parts of the island. With the leg bands intact, the bluebird team might be able to keep track of their movements.

I asked Kathleen if we knew where the bluebirds go in the winter. "We can only speculate," she replied. "We had a report via the identification from a leg band of them in the Willamette Valley in Oregon. We can only assume that they were drawn to that part of the state and into northern California. But generally, we still don't know exactly where our San Juan population goes."

Migration for many breeding birds in the San Juans was already underway but the bluebirds would remain into fall. "They linger like the last leaves on the tree," wrote naturalist Neltje Blanchan in *Birds Worth Knowing in* 1917. And so they do, much to our delight.

~

As usual, I got busy with other projects, but kept an eye on my calendar with thoughts of catching up with the blue moon birds before they fledged. I stopped at Red Mill briefly on August 16. The male was still taking grubs to the nest. All seemed well. I went back again, mid-morning on August 20. It was cool, about 60 degrees. Mist floated over the valley with the encouragement of a slight southeast breeze. My timing was perfect. Three newly fledged bluebirds were hanging out with the parents atop an old pear tree laden with ripe yellow fruit close to the Salish Seed Nursery. One nestling was still in the box on the split rail fence, leaning far out of the entrance hole screaming, I suspect, for food. Soon, the male obliged by taking insects to the holdout, but only staying briefly before returning to the tree tops to counsel the kids.

The adults were looking a bit scruffy. Their breeding plumage was worn; the fine lines of rust and blue were fading, signs the long breeding season was coming to an end—at least this phase of it. There was still much work to be done with the fledgling birds, including teaching them the still mysterious ways of this island world.

Young bluebirds and family groups would likely flock together before they headed south. American Camp, Mt. Finlayson and the gravel pit at Pear Point were among the favored late summer gathering places. The adults would stay with the juveniles through migration, and perhaps during the winter, before they separated ahead of the breeding season. Sometimes, offspring remained with their parents and returned together to San Juan Island the following spring. Kathleen was, of course, hoping some of the birds would overwinter on San Juan Island rather than migrating out of the area. Fingers crossed!

As often happens with these happy events, I was reluctant to leave Red Mill Farm that morning. Seeing the newly fledged birds using their blue wings was exhilarating. I had become invested in the life saga of the pair of breeding blues that had so diligently cared for two broods of chicks; I was relieved that the offspring had made it to flight. I held no illusions, however, that their futures were secure. For the moment, I was smiling. I headed back down the oak-lined driveway thinking of Dodie and ever grateful for her role in this successful saga. And so ended my auspicious first encounter with the western bluebirds.

~

It was December 20 and artist friend Nancy Spaulding and I headed out to celebrate winter solstice. We brought tea and tarts to sustain us as we scoured landscapes at Lime Kiln for winter visitors on the shortest day of the year. It had snowed modestly three days before, but moderated into a gray-white morning in the low 40s. An unpredictably upstart wind kept us guessing.

We began at Westside Lake a little before eleven o'clock and walked about only long enough for the clouds to spit light rain in our faces. The sun and the birds were nowhere to be found. We pondered a Plan B and I swung the car south along West Side Road as a cloud bank surged toward us across Haro Strait from Vancouver Island. The gray-green depths of the inland sea were rocking and rolling in the wind. The rain intensified as I stopped at the overview at Westside Preserve just as a red-tailed hawk peeled off in the wind.

"This is where I saw the bluebirds three weeks before," I told Nancy: "Six westerns skittering through the big-leaf maples along the grassy slope chattering softly to one another. There were still some berries on the madrones. I wonder if they could be …"

And, before I got the words out of my mouth, we both spotted the blues down by the bluff. It was pouring rain now. I turned on the windshield wipers to give us a better view. Yes, there were five, at least. They seemed to be riding the wind on the top, bare branches of a maple, but soon flushed and headed in our direction. They paused in another maple in front of the car park. What luck! They stayed only long enough for us to gasp and giggle at our good fortune. What could be better than finding western bluebirds in the rain on winter solstice. After a few more good looks, the blues were up and away. They were likely headed for cover in the nearby woods. We wondered where they had gone in the snow of a few days' past. Then, it was time to go.

I reflected later that, as an islander, I watched the beautiful birds leading wild lives in their historic realm, took heart at their perseverance—and ours—and knew that the world was still a place of possibilities. Thoreau asserted that the sweet bird: "… carried the sky on its back." I think the blue carries a few of our hopes for the future on its back, too. The Trust's bluebird project reminds us that sometimes—with a lot of hard work and a bit of luck—what seems lost may be found again. And so, we look optimistically toward a future of more bluebird springs.

Post Script: The news kept getting better for the bluebirds. In June 2022, Preservation Trust Conservation Project Manager Kathleen Foley Lewis announced that the Bluebird Project had experienced an exciting milestone. Trust volunteer Dan Clingaman spotted a western bluebird nesting in a natural cavity of a Garry oak tree on the island. Ross Lockwood got photographs. Kathleen commented: "We've been waiting for this moment throughout the history of the project. It's a HUGE and necessary step forward toward our goal of reintroducing a self-sustaining population of western bluebirds to this part of its northern range."

"In Ross's photos, the female is feeding her nestling, a juvenile pokes its head out of the hole, and the male is also present and contributing to the parental responsibilities."

Clingaman added: "I felt and shared her (Kathleen's) feeling of tearful joy that the birds had found and nested in a natural cavity after so many years of relying on boxes. The privilege of finding the bluebirds in the cavity was a true gift."

Weeks later, Kathleen added this note: "This prairie pair raised not just one batch of young, but two!" And so, the saga continues.

15

SEARCHING FOR SPRING

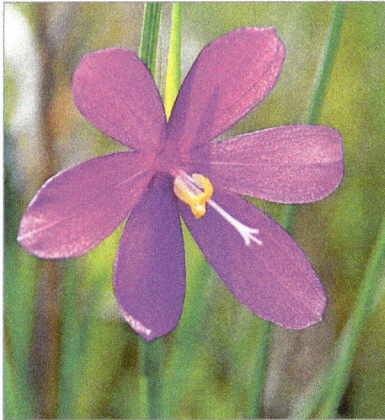

*This satin flower bloomed in late
February at Westside Preserve
after a winter storm. Could
spring be far away?*

I stood along the bluff at Westside Preserve after a hard rain counting the varied shades of gray and bedrock blue in Haro Strait and pondering the ashen sky. It was late February and I was getting restless. After months of dark clouds and relentless wind and rain, it was time to seek those first wildflowers of spring. Even though the vernal equinox was weeks away, I knew this was a likely spot to find the prize—if my timing was right.

A subtle seasonal shift was already underway. A pair of pigeon guillemots whistled their edgy, high-pitched mating calls just off-shore. The big-leaf maples boasted tight-fisted mahogany leaf buds soon to begin unfurling. And the western bluebirds I had seen here at winter solstice had moved on possibly scouting spring nesting sites elsewhere on the island.

The sun shone brightly—if briefly—upon the sixteen acres of gla-cially-tilled slopes. Just beneath the cold veneer, a wildflower awak-ening had begun. My old favorite satin flower—that sweet, seem-ingly frail, but most hardy of irises had slept through another island winter on these windswept slopes. Several of the plants' slender, bright green stalks had been breaking ground among the outcrops. Would this be the day of that first bloom?

There is an alluring air to the satin flower: modest in stature with a showy florescence. Its six-tepaled (tepals being undifferentiated petals and sepals) blooms perch atop twelve-inch stems with narrow, silvery-green, grass-like stem leaves. In bright sunlight, the pinkish-purple flowers cast a lustrous sheen, thus its name.

The plant thrives on grassy balds, knolls, rocky outcrops, and atop bluffs on cushions of bright green mosses and lichens, and in moist grassy meadows. Once uncommon on the island, the elegant blooms are increasingly evident from near the shoreline to the higher rockwork of Cady Mountain and Young Hill and flourish near Finlayson and the Redoubt at American Camp. Satin flower keeps company with a bright pink early blooming shooting star, often *Dodecatheon hendersonii*. Handsome goldback ferns with their shiny blackish-brown stipes also reside in the shallows of split-rock till near the satin gems at the Preserve. The miniscule, yellow *Mimulus alsinoides*—chickweed monkeyflower—is there, too.

Grass widow, satin flower and purple-eyed grass. These names court the beautiful iris. Its purplish-pink blossoms charmed early botanists. Scotsman David Douglas discovered it near Celilo Falls in the Columbia River Gorge in 1826. Botanist and photographer Dr. Lewis J. Clark wrote enthusiastically about satin flowers in *Wild Flowers of the Pacific Northwest*: "… reigning queen of the genus (*Sisyrinchium*). Indeed, a rock slope covered with these sprightly bells, sensitive to every whisper of wind, is one of the floral delights of early spring."

The scientific nomenclature has changed several times over nearly two hundred years. The current classification is *Olsynium douglasii var. douglasii*—a revision in genus from *Sisyrinchium* several years ago.

My pilgrimage to the preserve had become a yearly ritual often including the indispensable company of long-time islander, botanist extraordinaire, and dear friend Louisa Nishitani. We both loved the notion of finding that first blooming wildflower of the new year. Satin flower had never let us down, nor had Louisa's keen acuity that always found other treasures on the landscape to cheer our stay and broaden our minds. Over the years, Louisa had keyed out many of the grasses at the Preserve as a lasting reference for other plant-loving souls on the island. Alas, I was going it alone this year. My wildflower cohort Louisa had turned into her ninth decade and, while not up to navigating the steep slope, was eager to know what I found.

My search for satin flower did not take long. I turned my gaze from Haro Strait to the west-facing slope checking grassy edges and mossy outcrops for signs of *Sisyrinchium*. There would not be many yet, but surely at least a single bloom. Yes, there—on the landing under a big-leaf maple—a single, perfect flower. Considering the high wind gusts that had pounded this spot just days before, I marveled at the plant's perfection; I especially admired its magnificent magenta tepals fluttering in the brisk chill just above the sapphire sea. My timing was perfect. Here was my fortuneteller assuring me that spring was on the way. "Ah, satin flower. Welcome back!"

As I looked about, I saw several deep green shoots emerging from the moist, gritty soil. And up the hill, a fistful of fiery flowers. Oh, what was that? Several stalks already nibbled bare by the deer. Darn! But the sweet satin-finished iris survived—still glistening with raindrops. I was thrilled.

I took a few photographs for Louisa and started back up the slope. Wait—another one! It was tall and straight, and a paler shade of purple having emerged through a bed of silver and chartreuse mosses along a rock crevice. As always, Westside Preserve—and satin flower—had not let me down.

I would email Eliza and Doug at the Land Bank with the good news. Doug was the tireless steward of this spot and other LB preserves; his keen eyes often spied that first satin flower bloom at Deadman's Bay. And Eliza, master botanist, had for many years been collecting satin flower seeds—among other natives—for propagation. From a small pilot project, the Salish Seeds Nursery at Red Mill Farm was a resounding success. Satin flowers, spring gold, camas, columbine, red-flowering currant and a host of other native plants abound now in wild habitats and island gardens thanks to the important work by Eliza and her great team of volunteers. I knew both Doug and Eliza would be happy to hear the *Sisyrinchium* was now in bloom.

Thoroughly uplifted, I headed for town with photographs in hand to see my pal. Louisa's charming, white clapboard home was situated on a hilltop adjacent to Cattle Point Road with a spectacular east-facing view of Mt. Baker. Kulshan is the Lummi Indian name for the mountain.

The house, purchased in the late 1960s, was dubbed Thisbit Manor for the preponderance of thistle and rabbits that initially dominated the property. Now, the home was filled with books, photographs and memorabilia from a long and happy life with a devoted family and friends, and fond memories of her academic and professional achievements. Louisa was trained in botany by the renowned C. Leo Hitchcock during studies at the University of Washington. After a pause to join the WAVES during WW II, she returned to the UW and graduated Phi Beta Kappa. The decades that followed saw her richly involved in both her professional life and far-flung residents of her family. She was recognized for, among many accomplishments, her research on microscopic alga.

Louisa moved back permanently to Thisbit Manor in 2003 and devoted the rest of her life to conservation and stewardship issues here. Her tireless work was energized by countless friends and colleagues, and a deep kinship to our island home. Her teachings in botany, wildflower walks, and knowledge of local lore always brightened the times islanders spent with her. I especially enjoyed listening to her stories of early botanizing in the North Cascades, and our wildflower-seeking adventures on San Juan Island with Dr. Eugene Kozloff, one of the icons of Northwest natural history. Exploring in the field with Louisa and Koz was like taking a master class in flora and receiving an unspoken teaching in the generosity of spirit they both personified.

The modest, dark-eyed botanist with short-cropped hair lit up when she saw my images of satin flower from the Preserve. Louisa mused "Fantastic!!" in that soft, raspy song of a voice I knew so well. We sat at the kitchen table looking out across the bountiful open space, enjoying the presence of an extended family of California quail that had overwintered nearby, and speculating with great enthusiasm about the season forthcoming. With our favorite wildflower in bloom, we knew the shooting stars, common camas, field chickweed, prairie saxifrage and many more would not be far behind. Such a glorious time of year. No more steep slopes for Louisa, but plenty of smooth and flat places to explore with my wonderful friend. Not long after that, we drove down to American Camp to listen to the western meadowlarks singing in the grass before the yellow birds headed home from their winter respite on the plain. And, yes, there were satin flowers blooming there, too.

∼

Wildflowers speak to us in many ways. Perhaps it is not always as literal as the symbolic sheen of the little *Sisyrinchium* perched on a rocky knoll along the shelves of an ancient mountaintop, but still each flower tells a bit of the story of the character and natural history of the land.

Sometimes seeking our wildflower favorites with treasured friends has a symbolism of its own: a touchstone for enduring friendship and a shared acknowledgment of the awe-inspiring beauty in Nature and our deeply held commitments to keep the webs of life intact.

I wondered how satin flower perceived the howling wind hurtling in from the Pacific, the chirping of bald eagles overhead, the whistles of the guillemots, and the rain and snow seeping into the soil on frigid winter nights. Whatever the plant's power of perception, come late February or early March, the sweet flower emerged on the bluff and unfolded its rosy glow. Some years I caught a glimpse of that first unfurling; other times I did not. No matter to satin flower. The cycle of life continued and the sunshine was coming. That was reason enough for celebration. I knew Louisa would agree.

16

BIDDING ADIEU

"See you next fall, beautiful owl!"

The spring quickening had arrived. Since finding those first satin flowers on the wind-swept slopes of Westside Preserve in February, signs of the awakening began appearing on my walks about the island. Red-flowering currant burst into bloom at Third Lagoon. Skunk cabbage emerged from the muck at a Sitka spruce wetland. Tiny Soopolallie unfolded its miniscule yellow stars along the banks of Griffin Bay. Trumpeter swans gathered in San Juan Valley for their leave-taking to the Far North for the breeding season. Exuberant rufous hummingbirds arrived from southern climes, and orange-crowned warblers trilled from their perches high in the Douglas firs. All about, wildflowers and shrubs were stirring as slender threads of sunlight slowly transformed into midday sun streams that dispelled the clouds and warmed the softening March air. Indian plum, salmonberry, shooting stars, blue-eyed Mary and white-fawn lilies, among others, signaled the shift.

On March 3rd, I encountered my first butterfly of the new year. While walking down a lane near my home, the sun broke through gathered clouds and produced a splash of light at my feet. Just that fast, a mourning cloak fluttered out of the woods and alighted in the warming rays. "Old Cloak!" I exclaimed. "Here you are!" She was an old-timer; her rich maroon wings faded to a dusky brown, small blue wing spots rubbed away, and the creamy fringe frayed, torn and in tatters. But she had survived the winter, likely tucked away nearby behind the bark of an old evergreen, waiting for these short bursts of heat to fuel her solar-powered self. She wasn't inclined to move, but rather to absorb every bit of energy from the warming light. When clouds converged again, the old butterfly retreated into the woods, folding those worn wings against a tree trunk, and disappearing like magic into the conifer until another sunny spell. It would not be the last I would see of Cloak—or her kin—on the spring scape.

Also, near my cabin, I was cheered by the calls of yellow-rumped warblers. Ah, the yellow rumps. Since encountering their extraordinary migration event at The Labs in the fall, I eagerly awaited the songbirds' return for the breeding season. I spied two males high in a canopy of red alders, perch hunting for bugs. Their lilting call—a warm, whistled warble with a slight falling off at the end—had drawn my attention. The alders were just beginning to leaf out, and the soft gray, yellow and black birds were easy to spot. I suspected the duo had just arrived. Now, I knew, spring had finally come.

The arrival of spring meant the departure of the short-eared owls I had been watching all winter. It was just a year ago that I began this storytelling of wild lives on San Juan Island. "Sitting Still with Twilight Owls" was first. It only seems right to come full circle with their tale.

Last spring, the owls departed the island for their breeding grounds not long after the equinox. Some likely flew across the north Cascades to eastern Washington. While much of the owls' nesting habitat had been lost there to development or agricultural conversion, it was heartening to learn that in some places they were adapting to the new agrarian scheme and reproducing successfully.

The irrigated fields supported abundant small mammals and invertebrates favored by the owls. Then, come fall, a pair of short-eared owls appeared on our prairie as they had done for many years. I cannot say, of course, that it was the same pair that departed the previous spring, but the fact that the owls were still wintering here was cause for cheer.

Now, it was time to bid adieu to them again. It had been great fun observing them throughout the dark and rainy days of winter, but the seasonal shift was underway and time for them to go.

⁓

It was late afternoon, two days before the vernal equinox, when I arrived at American Camp. The weather was typical for this turn into spring: temperatures still in the high 30s, intermittent rain, remnant wind from a passing gale, sun breaks and shadows. The slanting gray light of the sun was beginning to gently fade across Haro Strait. It was blustery with winds gusting to 20 knots. The sky would soon be undone by clouds gathering over Vancouver Island and working their way east. White caps glistened silver off Salmon Bank. Short-cropped prairie grass read weary and worn from a long winter's rainy assault. I was glad I had donned a heavy jacket.

Eager to spot the owls, I settled in along the road edge north of the Witness Tree on Redoubt Road. I had a good view of the grassland without bothering the birds. It wasn't long before I spotted a short-eared owl far across the plain, several hundred yards away, just above Alaska Packer Rock. And soon, another owl. They were hunting along the upland trail adjacent to the willow thickets and freshwater spring by Salmon Bank Road. The thickets often hosted small songbirds this time of year including golden-crowned sparrows whose woeful call, characterized as "oh, dear me," seemed a commentary on the weather.

I watched the owls for some time. They navigated the vagaries of the wind, cruising just above the prairie grass to keep their balance and wheeling upslope to prowl the mid-section of the plain. The grassland was bound to the wind, and the owls were masters at using it. They flew headlong into the rush of wild air, at times nearly stalling over the scape in a perfect hover to scrutinize the grass. They cued on whatever moved, mostly mice and voles.

I was reminded of a passage from a classic bird book of long ago where an admiring biologist wrote about the owls' exceptional hearing: "Surely a Short-eared Owl could hear the footfall of a beetle at a hundred yards!" Even in the wind? I wondered

The wind had its own mind, dictating how wildlife moved in this habitat. Its endless energy seeped into every nook and cranny here and was part of the story of this land. Sometimes the wind seeped into my bones, too. I pulled the collar up on my jacket.

A northern harrier was there, as well, hunting in a customary zig-zag course over the grass sometimes crossing paths with the short-ies. This harrier was a male—slate gray above with dark wingtips, signature white rump patch, and light below. The hawk perfectly matched the color of the faded split rail fence he so often traversed while hunting. The male seemed sleeker than the buffy-brown female hawk—a much faster flyer than the owls. The raptors had the prairie to themselves. Neither the harrier nor the short-eared owls seemed in any hurry.

It was easy to be captivated by the engaging raptors: beautiful in form, fine in function. Prairie time always took over. I observed the moments between the owls' wingbeats, then timed how long they hovered before diving feetfirst into the grass. I listened to the cadence of bird calls and counted killdeer. I watched the slow passage of clouds across a pale winter sun. I waited for the next turn of the tide. Sometimes, the owls flew so close by that it took my breath away. It was a peaceful way of being.

I loved the way the owls looked with that perpetual surprised expression on their faces. Some called Owl a sorcerer, but the real magic was in her being exactly who she was and doing exactly what she had to do to retain her place on this competitive plain. Survival was not easy, especially in an age of changing landscapes and environmental conditions. Short-eared owls are creatures of habit and do not adapt well to change. They are nomads, wandering winter landscapes with their kin. In other areas of Washington State, the short-eared owl population had plummeted. Yet, the shorties kept coming back to the island while all around seemed in transition. Owl persevered.

Owl was my teacher. She showed me something about herself, about the prairie, and about myself every time I saw her. Independent yet connected. Watching her reminded me of how grateful I was to live on San Juan Island. I wondered what Owl would show me next.

~

I saw no sign of Shrike and heard no bubbling songs from the western meadowlarks. I suspected the larks were keeping company with the grass until the wind died down. Northern flickers were there, as well. Their preferred perch was an old elderberry bush sprouting out of the split in a large glacial erratic down the road—but there was no resting in the wind today.

The stiff Salish breeze finally subsided. Crows appeared down by Pickett's Lane and began their own version of hunting strategy. They lined up six abreast in the short grass and strutted toward the western shore kicking up tiny morsels to feed their willful ways.

~

I looked again for the owls but they were gone. It did not stay quiet for long. A mature bald eagle flew in from the east and took a perch atop the Witness Tree. The eagle was a full-time resident, likely one of a mated pair that nested nearby in a grove of Douglas firs. It was common to see the balds returning to the nest site in the spring from fishing in the straits.

I turned away from the bald, then heard a loud, raspy scream coming from above the old tree. I looked back to see a red-tailed

Red-tailed Hawk (dark morph).

hawk knock the eagle off its perch. They both flew up and away. An encounter ensued with the much bigger eagle literally rolling onto its back in the air with talons extended defending against the smaller, faster and agile hawk. The red-tail did a somersault of sorts and a strike while taunting the bald. *Kee-eeee-ar!* it screamed in two, long slow, descending notes. It continued to shriek at the immense bird as they flew toward the conifers to the east.

A flicker, downslope, delivered a spirited *yuk yuk yuk* admonition to the pair for disturbing its peace.

I had observed similar encounters several weeks before—the hawk screaming at the eagle over that grove of firs. Red-tails are territorial birds. I suspected it had a nest-site in mind in that vicinity, too. Not a great location, perhaps.

I was glad to have witnessed the drama. It occurred to me I had taken red-tailed hawks for granted. I had observed them all my life most often perched by the side of the road on fence posts scanning the surroundings for prey. I remember taking road trips with my family as a young girl and counting red-tailed hawks along the way.

I still do that when I am driving on the mainland—keeping count of the red-tails as I pass through the Skagit Flats. Alas, I had never taken time to watch them extensively other than to note in my field journal their presence and behaviors. I was glad they were there, of course, but the unassuming red-tails lacked the drama of the balds and peregrines to sustain my attention. Now, the hawk screaming at the bald and knocking it off its perch: that was drama! She was angry and magnificent. Her red tail shouted her identity. Hello, Hawk!! I thought. I felt I was seeing her with fresh eyes.

On the island, I often saw the red-tails soaring high above making those lazy circles biologists and songwriters have mused over for ages. My favorite passage about red-tailed hawks comes from the early 19th century *Birds of Washington*: "… the wonder of flight, the beauty and the witchery of those lazy, high-flung circles. How consonant with sunshine and shimmering air and anon, with peace itself, are those mystic circles of endless, unimpassioned quest!"

The red-tail screamed for several minutes at the bald now perched high in the conifers past the Parade Grounds. Eventually, the eagle flew toward July Beach with the hawk in pursuit. It grew quiet on the plain once more.

∽

As I waited for the owls to return, I pondered the small patch of grassland that I had visited regularly for many years. While I would be sorry to see the owls leave, I knew the months ahead promised many welcome events: breeding songbirds, blooming native wildflowers, fluttering butterflies, fledgling bald eagles, rambunctious fox kits, shorebirds in fall migration, and so much more.

The diversity and abundance of flora and fauna at the south end of the island had changed dramatically over time. Species had come and gone. Remember skylark? The web of life was showing signs of fraying whether from natural processes or human impacts. San Juan is an island, after all. It has edges. And those edges create boundaries. It was getting crowded. The quiet places for sitting still and watching wildlife were fewer, farther between, and more remote.

I took a moment to acknowledge the keepers of the web of life on the prairie. Most led unnoticed lives yet held the slender threads of numerous microhabitats together. The fragile configurations kept the balance of Nature intact. Each species was the custodian of a unique niche. Indispensable.

The owls, hawks and eagles I had seen that day were perhaps the most visible keepers of this plain, but no more important than the rest of the natives—especially the pollinators—in their value to the health and longevity of this ecosystem. Even the dreaded Canada thistle had its role to play although, I had to admit, there is too much of it now. I shall continue, though, to advocate for leaving some thistle patches intact as prairie restoration projects progress. It is important in late summer and fall to butterflies, to goldfinch before they depart, and to late migrating sparrows, among others, who count on thistle for shelter against gathering Pacific storms.

Over time, I had heard many voices on the prairie: the songs of reverie of savannah sparrows on a spring morning, the deep-throated hoots of great horned owls in the middle of the night, the cackle of crows, the chatters and peals of bald eagles, the chirping of grasshoppers that fed the migrating hoards each late summer and early fall, the bark of red foxes, and the bleats of black-tailed deer. These voices were signs of life, diversity, continuity, and belongingness to this place. Yes, change was happening, but the soul of the prairie remained intact.

~

The short-eared owls returned and my attention was brought back to the plain, but alas, it was time to go. Walking back to the car, my leave-taking was interrupted when a young bald eagle careened in over the ridge from Griffin Bay, flying low across the road just past the Witness Tree toward the owls. It was a second-year bird—chocolate brown above with white mottling on its chest, and distinct white plumes on its underwings and tail. I heard every stroke of its heavy wingbeats passing by and saw the feathers on its neck stiffen. Its light brown eyes were fixed in the owls' direction.

The eagle's abrupt arrival unsettled the owls. One hastened up the slope toward the Redoubt. The harrier veered off, as well. The second short-eared owl held her space in the shadow of the much bigger bird. She barked three times at the aggressor and made a bold move toward it—talons out and feathers ruffled. The eagle made a mid-course correction, turning sharply away, but soon flew back to face the owl. The raptors hovered and circled over the plain. The eagle advanced. The shortie did not relent. They rose together with a flurry of wingbeats—eye to eye—jousting for position and nearly brushing one another's wingtips.

The prairie owl held the high ground in the sky but soon seemed to grasp her vulnerability. She split the crisp air with her soft wings heading through layers of colorless sky toward gathering cumulus clouds above. The eagle stayed on her tail. Relentless! I could still hear the owl's barking chants—louder, more determined. The young aggressor did not make a sound.

Finally, the owl was only a tiny, white-feathered spot in the sky disappearing into that cloud canopy. The eagle retreated over the ridge to Old Town.

What an extraordinary chase! I had never seen an owl fly to such heights. I knew Owl still had things to show me. I did not expect it to be something so spectacular.

I waited and watched the sky. A few minutes passed before the second owl—noting the eagle's retreat—glided back down the slope from the Redoubt and perched on the high ground of a large, lichen-covered erratic. The harrier resumed his prowl over the freshwater spring by Alaska Packer Rock. The eagle did not return—at least, not yet.

The sun broke through the gathering clouds washing the edge of the plain with a column of golden light. I continued to glance skyward looking for the brave owl. No luck. And, it was time to head home. I started back down the road disappointed at not getting one last look at Owl. But, wait! Here she came, having descended out of the overcast and quickly resuming her measured flight along the grassy fence line next to the road. She was headed northwest and, as luck would have it, right into that beam of late afternoon sun. Owl shone gold in the scattered, glistening sheen. She stroked into a gentle breeze; wide, soft wings wavering slightly; earnest gaze fixed on the quickening scape where the first wildflowers of spring were stirring. It was nearing twilight and there was work to be done.

It was the perfect way to end my visit. All was well as the steadfast shortie reclaimed her place on the awakening plain. Would I ever truly know Owl? Of course, not. While the entirety of her world was an enigma to me, my encounters, however brief, remained touchstones in my naturalist's life on San Juan Island. I kept watching out of admiration and curiosity, and in the hope that the few small things I learned about short-eared owls might help keep this place safe and intact so they could return another day. Ultimately, to know Owl is to respect her wildness, her space, and her place in our shared world.

I lingered a few moments more as Owl flew out of sight up the fence line toward the Redoubt. I bid her a fond adieu and safe journey. "See you next fall, beautiful owl!"

Notes

Preface

P. 11 faint yellow throats: There are two subspecies of yellow-rumped warblers (*Dendroica coronata*) found in Washington State. They are distinguished by subtle marking differences and distribution. The Myrtle form has a white throat and lacks white patches between its white wing bars. It mostly migrates through the islands and is a winter visitor here. The Audubon form has a yellow throat and commonly breeds in the islands as well as in northern coniferous forests sometimes at high altitudes. It was the Audubon subspecies I encountered at The Labs. <birdweb.org/BIRDWEB/bird/yellow-rumped_warbler>.

Sitting Still With Twilight Owls

P. 19 short-eared owl: *Asio flammeus* is a species of true owls in the Family Strigidae. It was first described by Pontoppidan in 1763 and is one of the most widely distributed owls on Earth ranging on every continent but Australia and Antarctica and inhabiting many oceanic island groups such as the Galapagos and Hawaii. Asio is the genus of eared owls, and flammeus is Latin for "flaming" or "the color of fire" that refers to the luster of its plumage in bright light.

P.19 short-eared owl: Washington State Department of Wildlife website identifies the short-eared owl as a Species of Greatest Conservation Need (SGCN) under the State Wildlife Action Plan (SWAP) on their website: <https://wdfw.wa.gov/species-habitats/

species/asio-flammeus#conservation>. Accessed online March 30, 2022.

P. 21 "Marsh owl, swamp owl …": Pearson, T. Gilbert (Editor in Chief). 1917. *Birds of America*. The University Society, Inc.: New York. Part II, p. 101.

P. 23 possibly in fallow fields: According to the Washington Department of Fish and Wildlife, short-eared owls are found breeding (among other places) in: "… dunes, old fields. grassy plains, and prairies in eastern Washington … In western Washington, they appear to be scarce or absent in many areas where they used to be, such as in estuaries, prairies and coastal dunes." <https://wdfw.wa.gov/species-habitats/species/asio-flammeus#conservation>. Retrieved online March 30, 2022.

P. 24 changed again: Avery, Christy. 2016. *San Juan Island National Historical Park – An Environmental History*. U.S. National Park Service, Pacific West Regional Office, Seattle, Washington. This book offers an excellent summary of land use and development at American Camp.

P. 24 Mark Lewis documented: Lewis, Mark and Fred A. Sharpe. 1987. *Birding in the San Juan Islands*. The Mountaineers: Seattle. Note 70, p. 203.

P. 24 if not breeding residents: I photographed a short-eared owl from the Redoubt at American Camp foraging in the grassland below on May 26, 2012.

P. 25 Eurasian skylark … first sighting on San Juan: Lewis & Sharpe. 1987. Note 83, p. 204.

P. 25 original documentation of that first sighting: James A. Bruce: "First Record of European Skylark on San Juan Island, Washington", *The Condor*, Volume 63, Issue 5, September 1961, p. 418, https://doi.org/10.1093/condor/63.5.418.

P. 26 meadowlarks: Lewis & Sharpe. 1987. Note 117, p. 206-07.

P. 26 Susan Fenimore Cooper: Cooper, Susan Fenimore. 1850. *Rural Hours*. George P. Putnam, Putnam's American Agency: New York. Entry from June 30th.

P. 26 Was that a skylark: My last encounter with the skylark; from SV Journal, Vol A1; March 6, 1998.

P. 27 "... rather stupid ...": Pearson. 1917. Part II p. 102.

P. 27 rabbit-proof fence: In the early to mid-2000s, a fence was installed from Redoubt Road west across the grassland toward South Beach, in part, as an attempt to control European rabbits; it was taken down likely in 2016. Its presence appeared most valuable to birds from shrikes and sparrows to raptors who routinely used it for perch hunting.

Salish Blues

P. 29 western tailed blue butterfly: *Cupido amyntula* is a species of true-blue butterflies in the Family Lycaenidae. It was first described by French lepidopterist Jean Baptiste Boisduval in 1852. The blue commonly ranges from Alaska, through most of the Canadian provinces, down through the western United States to northern Baja, California. It is found in both eastern and western Washington from the mountains to the shore. Pyle, Robert Michael. 2002. *The Butterflies of Cascadia*. p. 226.

P. 32 western bluebirds were breeders: Lewis & Sharpe. 1987. p.171, Note 93, p. 205.

P. 32 successful reintroduction program: San Juan Preservation Trust; <https://sjpt.org/news/western_bluebird/>.

P. 32 Mountain bluebirds: Lewis & Sharpe. 1987. Note 94, p. 205.

P. 32 "... little blue herald ...": Blanchan, Neltje. 1897. *Bird Neighbors*. Garden City Publishing Inc.: Garden City, New Jersey. p. 99.

P. 32 predictable succession: This succession of plant blooms will be variable depending on the habitat, elevation, seasonality, etc.

P. 33 near Alaska Packer Rock: The rock is a prominent outcrop below the freshwater spring along Salmon Bank Road at South Beach. The icon is named after the Alaska Packers Association (APA) a late 19th and early 20th century organization that combined salmon-packing operations in Alaska and southward into a highly influential entity. They had a presence at South Beach into the 1920s when the association merged into the California Packing Corporation (CalPack). Pratt, Boyd. (2021) *ISLAND FISHING - History and Seascape of Marine Harvesting in the San Juan Islands Amid the Salish Sea.* Mulno Cove Publishing: Friday Harbor, p. 180.

P. 34 I had raised their eggs: Vernon, Susan. 2014. *Rescue, Rearing and Release of the Island Marble Butterfly (Euchloe ausonides insulanus)* on San Juan Island, Washington, 2009-2010. Unpublished report for Washington State Department of Wildlife.

P. 36 blues' life cycle: James David G. and David Nunnallee. 2011. *Life Histories of Cascadia Butterflies*, Oregon State University Press: Corvallis, pp. 186-187.

Vireo Spring

P. 41 *Zeedle, zeedle*: Characterization from *All About Birds* website: https://www.allaboutbirds.org/guide/Black-throated_Gray_Warbler/sounds; accessed 09-13-22.

P. 42 four species found: Hutton's vireo, warbling vireo, red-eyed vireo, and Cassin's vireo. Lewis & Sharpe. 1987. p.172.

P. 42 "… white spectacles …": Sibley, David. 2000. *The Sibley Guide to Birds.* Alfred A, Knopf: New York, p. 349.

P. 42 "… sings as he works …": Dawson, W.L. & J.H Bowles. 1909. *Birds of Washington, A Complete Scientific and Popular Account of the 372 Species of Birds Found in the State.* Seattle Occidental Pub Co. p. 365.

P. 43 Yes, it was a Cassin's: *Vireo cassinii* is a songbird from the Family Vireoidae. It was first described in 1858, named for 19th century American ornithologist John Cassin.

P. 43 Cassin's vireo: Goguen, B. and D. R. Curson, 2002. Cassin's Vireo (*Vireo cassinii*), version 2.0. In *The Birds of North America* (A. F. Poole and F. B. Gill, Editors). Cornell Lab of Ornithology, Ithaca, NY, USA. <https://doi.org/10.2173/bna.615> This paper is an excellent resource for Cassin's vireo.

P. 44 was excavated in the 1970s: Domico, Terry. 1998. *Lime Kiln Quarries Property, San Juan Island, San Juan County, Washington*. Puget Sound BioSurvey: Seattle, WA. p. 12.

P. 44 Buck's Pond: Domico. 1998. p. 12.

P. 44 Limekiln Preserve: Online summary of Limekiln Preserve and Westside Lake at <https://sjclandbank.org/portfolio-items/limekiln-preserve-and-westside-lake/>.

P. 45 Westside Lake: The number of species and abundance of individual waterfowl overwintering at Westside Lake appeared to have declined in the 2022-2023 seasons. Preserve Steward Doug McCutchen is investigating possible causes of this decline with local and regional wildlife officials and water quality experts. Increased monitoring of the site may produce important data to clarify the current impression of paucity.

P. 45 rustic bird blind: Residents on the west side of San Juan Island constructed the blind along Westside Lake in the early 2000s. It has become a popular site for locals to observe winter waterfowl, especially common mergansers, ring-necked ducks, American wigeons, green-winged teal and others.

P. 47 time for fledging: Incubation: 12-14 days; fledge: nestling period 12-14 days; total days egg to flight: 24-30 days. From *All About Birds*: <https://www.allaboutbirds.org/guide/Cassins_Vireo/lifehistory>.

P. 48 Edward Howe Forbush: *Birds of America*. 1917. T. Gilbert Pearson ed. Garden City Publishing Company: Garden City, New York. Part III, p. 107.

P. 48 woodland relatively intact: The San Juan County Conservation Land Bank manages the Limekiln Preserve.

Rock Garden

P. 53 The story of industrializing: Pratt, Boyd C. 2014. *Limestone Quarrying and Limemaking in the San* Juan *Islands*, HistoryLink.org 10935, accessed 9/26/18. An excellent overview of Lime Kiln history.

P. 55 microhabitats: Domico. 1998, *Site Assessment for Priority Habitats and Species of Concern Lime Kiln Quarries Property, San Juan Island, San Juan County, Washington.* pp. 1-25.

P. 56 Coughlan's Trail: personal communication with Doug Mc-Cutchen. August 10, 2021.

P. 57 limestone-bearing: Domico. 1998. p. 18.

P. 57 completed in 2016: The connector trail was built by a great crew from the American Hiking Society's Volunteer Vacations program, added Doug McCutchen, 2021.

P. 57 broad-leaved stonecrop: *Sedum spathulifolium* is a perennial succulent herb of the Family Crassulaceae. It was first described by Hooker. The highly visible native is found on rocky outcrops, cliffs, bluff and forest openings at low to medium elevations. It ranges from British Columbia down the west coast of America to southern California.

P. 57 flat-topped clusters: Pojar, Jim and Andy MacKinnon. 2004. *Plants of the Pacific Northwest Coast, Washington, Oregon, British Columbia & Alaska.* Lone Pine Publishing: Vancouver, British Columbia. p. 155.

P. 58 sedeo "to sit": Clark, Lewis J. 1976. *Wild Flowers of the Pacific Northwest*, Gray's Publishing Limited: Sidney, British Columbia Canada. p. 197.

P. 58 "… cast-iron constitution …": Clark. 1976. p. 200.

P. 58 "… low spreading canopy …": Ibid.

P. 58 "a favored perch …": Clark. 1976. p. 204.

P. 58 *Saxifraga cespitosa*: Eliza Habegger, personal communication, June 2017.

P. 58 tufted saxifrage: *Saxifraga cespitosa* is a perennial of the Family Saxifrage. It was first described by Linnaeus in 1753. It is found in rocky crevices, ledges, talus slopes and outcrops. The wide-ranging herb is common at sea level to alpine tundra from Norway, Iceland, Greenland and Siberia (among others) to western United States.

P. 60 Ranger David Halpern: personal communication, David Halpern, August 25, 2021 at Lime Kiln Point State Park.

P. 62 the light gray stone: Pratt, Boyd C. 2016. *LIME, Quarrying and Lime Making in the San Juan Islands.* Mulno Cove Publishing: Friday Harbor. p. 1.

P. 63 Moss' elfin: Pyle. 2002. p. 216.

Mona's World

P. 67 Pacific sideband snail: *Monadenia fidelis* is a terrestrial mollusk of the Family Bradybaenidae. It was first described by J.E. Gray in 1834.

P. 67 I first met Mona: Vernon, Susan. 2010, *Rainshadow World*, Archipelago Press: Friday Harbor, WA p. 63.

P. 69 love darts: Grebowski, Pete, Nature's Cupid: the Pacific Sideband Snail, <www.nisquallylandtrust.org/natures-cupid-the-pacific-sideband-snail/.

P. 69 long naps in dry summers: snails are found deep in talus accumulations which are adjacent to springs or streams and serve as refuge sites from desiccation and protection from predators.

Night Life

P. 71 sand-verbena moth: *Copablepharon fuscum* is a species of moth of the Order Lepidoptera and belongs to the second largest family of owlet moths (Noctuidae) in the world. It was first described by Troubridge and Crabo in 1995.

P. 74 yellow sand-verbena: *Abronia latifolia* is a member of the Four-o'clock Family (Nyctaginaceae). It was first described by Eschscholtz. The hairy, tap-rooted perennial is native to the west coast of North America from British Columbia to California prominent, in some areas, on coastal dunes and back beaches. Its population is declining in part because of the invasion of non-native plant species, recreational activity along dunes and land development. Its stout roots were historically eaten by the Chinook.

P. 74 since 1995: Troubridge, JT and LG Crabo. 1995. "A new species of *Copablepharon* (Lepidoptera: Noctuidae) from British Columbia and Washington." *Journal of the Entomological Society of British Columbia* 92:87-90.

P. 76 significant field work: Gibble, W. and JW Fleckenstein. 2013. *Copablepharon fuscum* (sand-verbena moth) and *Abronia latifolia* (yellow sand-verbena) Washington State Surveys. Washington Natural Heritage Program: Olympia, WA. 27pp.

P. 84 Cattle Point: Fleckenstein, J.W. Combs, J.K., Thorpe, A.S. 2018a. Survey of Known and Potential Sites of the Sand-verbena Moth (*Copablepharon fuscum*). Washington Natural Heritage Program, Olympia: WA. 21pp.

American Avocet & the Long-Ago Lagoon

P. 89 American avocet *Recurvirostra americana* is a shorebird of the Family Recurvirostridae. It was first described in 1789 by Gmelin. The large wader inhabits saline lakes and marshes in the Pacific Northwest and winters along the southern coast of the United States and western Mexico. Thousands of avocets congregate and breed near the Klamath lakes in Oregon and are common spring and summer visitors to the Columbia Basin in eastern Washington, as well. They are noisy, gregarious birds usually found traveling in flocks.

P. 89 The American Avocet: Paulson, Dennis. 1993. *Shorebirds of the Pacific Northwest*. University of Washington Press: Seattle. pp. 138-141.

P. 89 having been recorded twice: Lewis & Sharpe.1987. page 202; entry no. 44. Two records. S. Atkinson found one at Richardson Ponds on both 17 and 18 June 1980. M. Mallea located three at Swift Bay Pond 26 May 1987.

P. 91 "blue shank" or "blue stocking …": Pearson, T. Gilbert (Editor in Chief). 1917. *Birds of America*. The University Society, Inc.: New York. Part I, p. 222.

P. 91 Wolves roamed: *Journal of Charles Griffin, Belle Vue Farm Post Journals*, Microfilm: 1M16 HBC call # B.15/a/1-Post Journal from 1854-55. This section transcribed by Boyd C. Pratt/ January 2002.

P. 91 Salmon salting station: Vouri, Mike. 2008. *The Pig War*. Arcadia Publishing: Charleston, South Carolina. p. 9.

P. 92 A painting by James Madison Alden: Schroeder, Tom. 2007. *Rediscovering A Coastal Prairie Near Friday Harbor*, <http://www.rockisland.com/~tom?LostPrairie.html>; p. 12. A water-color painting from 1859. The ships shown are the HMS *Satellite* and U.S. Coast Survey Ship *Active* in Griffin Bay just off Old Town Lagoon.

P. 93 "the scalawags": *Journal of Charles Griffin, Belle Vue Farm Post Journals*, Microfilm: 1M16 HBC call # B.15/a/1-Post Journal from 1854-55.

P. 94 saltmarsh dodder: Kozloff, Eugene N. 1983. *Seashore Life of the North Pacific Coast*. University of Washington Press: Seattle. pp. 339-341.

P. 94 field class: Salt Marsh Ecosystem with Dr. Eugene N. Kozloff. June 19, 1999 at Jakle's Lagoon.

P. 94 Grande Bay: *Belle Vue Sheep Farm Post Journals*, 1859. Footnote 25. This is the first reference to Griffin Bay, formerly "Grande Bay" and "Belle Vue Bay." Transcribed by Boyd C. Pratt. https://www.nps.gov/sajh/learn/historyculture/upload/Griffin-Journal-1859-2.pdf.

P. 98 especially when one has no choice: With a bow to *The Snow Leopard* by Peter Matthiesson (1978). PM and Jang-bu encounter the Lama at the Crystal Monastery (November 14). He appears to be a happy man in spite of physical affliction that will not allow his leaving the Himalayan mountainside. When asked why he is happy, the Lama replies: "Of course I am happy here! It's wonderful! *Especially* when I have no choice!"

Note: Years ago, when I saw the avocet at Old Town Lagoon, I was not aware that a little white butterfly (thought to be extinct since 1908) was seeking the safety of this brackish world using *Lepidium virginicum* as its host plant. I had settled in the drift to watch the shorebirds and been so absorbed that I may not have noticed the island marble butterfly fluttering along the shoreline with the ever-present cabbage whites we all know and generally dismiss.

Keeper of the Seasons

P. 99 northern red-legged frog: *Rana aurora aurora is* a member of the Family of True Frogs. It was first described in 1852 by Baird and Girard. It is the largest native western frog and is common on the coast from southern British Columbia to northern California but may not be common in the San Juans.

P. 102 Coast Salish lore: Stonington Gallery, June Report. "Spotlight on Frogs." <https://stoningtongallery.com/exhibit/spotlight-on-frogs/>.

P. 103 Frog is also the messenger: <http://uvac.uvic.ca/gallery/cornett/artword/frog. A photo caption for a work by Andy Peterson entitled *Frog.*

P. 104 series of call notes: Sibley, David. 2000. *The Sibley Guide to Birds.* Alfred A, Knopf: New York. p. 383.

P. 106 fern prairie: Schroeder, Tom, 2007. "Rediscovering A Coastal Prairie Near Friday Harbor," <http://www.rockisland.com/~tom?LostPrairie.html>; p. 3.

P. 106 open land covered with: Ibid.

P. 106 the land was occupied: Ibid. p. 1.

P. 106 designated a military reserve: Ibid. p. 3.

P. 106 Schroeder did exhaustive research: Ibid. p. 1.

P. 106 historic photographs taken: Ibid. pp. 13 of 20.

P. 106 "It seemed reasonable to assume": Schroeder. 2007. p. 9.

P. 108 Central America: The Cornell Lab. All About Birds. Swainson's Thrush/range map. <https://www.allaboutbirds.org/guide/swainson's_thrush/maps-range>.

One Small Patch

P. 113 pearly everlasting: *Anaphalis margaritacea is a* species of woody flowering plant within the Family Asteracea. The genus was first described in 1838 by deCandolle and deCandolle. And species in 1873 by (L.) Benth. & Hook, f. The rhizomatous plant is native to North America and found from alpine sites to the sea. It blooms at lower elevations in late summer and early fall.

P. 114 curl its agile tool: Pyle, Robert Michael. 1992. *Handbook for Butterfly Watchers*, Houghton Mifflin Company: Boston, p. 20.

P. 114 Archibald Menzies: Newcombe, C.F. 1923. *Menzies' Journal of Vancouver's Voyage*. Archives of British Columbia, Victoria, B.C. Appendix, p. 133.

P. 114 "... dry and unwithering ...": Dana, Mrs. William Starr, *How to Know the Wild Flowers*, first published by Charles Scribner's Sons in 1893; copyright 1989 by Houghton Mifflin Company, p. 65.

P. 115 Mrs. William Starr Dana: Sierra College website; *Journal of the Sierra College Natural History Museum*. Frances Theodora Parsons: <https://www.sierracollege.edu/ejournals/jscnhm/v6n1/parsons.html> Accessed, November 16, 2021; *How to Know the Ferns* was Parson's last nature book. In the ensuing years, Parsons turned her attention to supporting women's suffrage and later politics.

P. 116 Amy suggested: Dr. Amy Lambert, personal communication. April 19, 2017.

P. 117 "… one of the great survivors of the urban scape …": of purplish copper, Robert Michael Pyle, *The Butterflies of Cascadia*, Seattle Audubon: Seattle. p. 182.

P. 117 American Lady: Kurt and Eleanor McMillan, personal communication, September 2004. Also known as American Painted Lady.

P. 118 admirals migrating: October 25, 2010, American Camp to Cattle Point NRCA; Vernon. 2010. pp. 74-77.

P. 118 "Thou canst not stir a flower …": Francis Thompson, (1859-1907) from his poem "The Mistress of Vision" in *The Works of Francis Thompson* published by Burns Oates.

Long-Distance Dragons

P. 121 variegated meadowhawk: *Sympetrum corruptum* is of the Family Libellulidae. It was first described in 1861 by Hagen. The skimmers are widespread in America, especially in the West. Its range includes British Columbia to Nova Scotia and south to Mexico; also known in the Russian Far East. In Washington State, meadowhawks are encountered from early May to early November. Its preferred habitats are ponds, lakes and slow-moving streams.

P. 128 *Dragonflies of Washington*: Dennis Paulson, *Dragonflies of Washington*. 1999. Seattle Audubon Society, p. 28.

P. 130 "Dragonflies Swarm Cannon Beach …": Town News. *Cannon Beach Gazette*, Cannon Beach, OR. 2 September 7, 2010.

P. 130 "Mass Flights of Dragonflies create Awe on Oregon Coast …": <https://www.beachconnection.net/news/dragfl090710_536.php>. 09/07/2010. *Oregon Coast Beach Connection*.

P. 130 Tweeters Birding Email: 2 September, 2010. Tokeland Dragonfly Migration—just started; [Grad, Andrea E.] followed up by Paulson.

P. **130** Dr. Dennis Paulson: Director Emeritus, University of Puget Sound. *Dragonflies and Damselflies of the West*, Princeton University Press: Princeton. 2009. pp. 457-59.

P. 130 "This movement …": Dennis Paulson, personnel communications, September 5–20, 2010.

P. 131 "… mostly migrate over land …": Ibid.

P. 132 No one knows: And, one more theory about the migration. "Dragonflies on the Oregon Coast: An Annual Event." *Sympetrum corruptum* is present year- round in the south and southwest U.S. and in Mexico. The surmise is that they might migrate diffusely north in the summer, where they breed in warm areas away from the coast, then fly or get blown across the Coast Range mountains on the strong east winds in late summer. Reaching the ocean, they head south back to their year-round range. Since no one has managed to follow the flights in a systematic way, this is just speculation. If variegated meadowhawks became as popular as monarch butterflies, with people watching out for them throughout the west, perhaps we would be able to piece together more of the story." Reported in *What We Surmise* – COASTWATCH – SEPTEMBER 14, 2010 by Terry Morse.

P. 132 nearly three hundred million years: Fossil remains tell us that, long ago, dragonflies had wingspans of nearly three feet. In Asia and the Americas, dragonflies are considered symbols of good luck although folklore about "eye pokers" and "the devil's darning needle" still resonates with some folks. Some Native Americans consider them messengers of wisdom and symbols of change. Long ago in Europe and Australia, they were more often demonized.

P. 132 "… O, brief, bright smile of summer …": Celia Thaxter in her poem "Already in Drift-Weed". 1878. p. 103.

Walking With Pipits
P. 135 American pipit: *Anthus rubescens* is a songbird of the Family Motacillidae. It was described by Marmaduke Tunstall in 1771.

Also know as buff-bellied pipit. Pipits are found on both sides of the North Pacific and common in the North American west. They breed on the Alaska and Canadian tundra and alpine meadows into the Pacific Northwest. While common, these songbirds are declining due to habitat loss and climate factors.

P. 141 "… nomads …": Dawson, W.L. & J.H Bowles. 1909. *Birds of Washington, A Complete Scientific and Popular Account of the 372 Species of Birds Found in the State.* Seattle Occidental Pub Co. No. 90. American Pipit, p. 222.

P. 143 Salmon Bank: Wray, Jacilee, *The Salmon Bank, An Ethnohistoric Compilation* by Jacilee Wray, (2003). This is a fine resource for learning about Salmon Bank on San Juan.

P. 143 geologic formation: San Juan Island National Historic Park (U.S. National Park Service), The Salmon Bank at South Beach, <https://www.nps.gov/sajh/learn/historyculture/south-beach-on-the-salmon bank.htm> p. 2.

P. 143 "… best fishing grounds …": *Geographical Memoir of the Islands Between the Continent and Vancouver Island in the Vicinity of the Forty-Ninth Parallel of North Latitude*; October 1868; 40th Congress, 2nd Session, Ex Doc No. 29 by Archibald Campbell, Appendix A. Report of Dr. C.B.R Kennerly Surgeon and Naturalist, of a Reconnaissance of Orcas Island, December 29, 1857, p. 13.

P. 144 fish traps: Pratt, Boyd C. 2021. *Island Fishing, History and Seascape of Marine Harvesting in the San Juan Islands amid the Salish Sea*, Mulno Cove Publishing: Friday Harbor, pp. 60-80.

P. 144 tent village: Avery, Christy. 2016. *San Juan Island National Historic Park - An Environmental History,* National Park Service, U.S. Dept of the Interior. p. 92.

Seeker of Wandering Stones

P. 151 northern shrike: *Lanius borealis* is a predatory songbird of the Family Laniidae. It was first described in 1808 by Viellot.

Shrikes breed in northern tundra and taiga and winter in southern Canada and the northern United States. The species was originally named *L. excubitor*, Latin for butcher watchman or sentinel.

P. 152 butcher bird, nine killer: Pearson. 1917. Part III. p. 99.

P. 153 "... scric ...": Old English meaning: From Old Norse *skrikja* ("to scream") or Old English *scric*, literally "bird with a shrill call," referring to a thrush, possibly imitative of its call. <https://www.yourdictionary.com/shrike>.

P. 153 "Not even a hawk itself ...": Neltje Blanchan, *Bird Neighbor*. 1897. Garden City Publishing Inc.: Garden City, New Jersey. p. 88.

P. 153 assassin: Burroughs, John. 1887. *Locust and Wild Honey*. Houghton Mifflin, Riverside Press: Boston.VI. Birds and Birds.

P. 153 "... *All times are killing* ...": Dawson, William Leon and John Hooper Bowles. 1909. Volume 1 of 2. No. 135. p. 354.

P. 155 errare: <https://www.vocabulary.com/dictionary/erratic>; derived from the Latin verb *errare*, or "to wander" off course. In geology, an erratic is a rock not native to a specific place but transported there by glacial activity.

P. 156 almost pyriform: Baicich, Paul J. and Colin J.O. Harrison. 1997. *A Guide to the Nests, Eggs, and Nestlings of North American Birds* (Second Edition), Academic Press: San Diego. p. 126.

P. 156 the Redoubt: The Redoubt. National Park Service/U.S. Department of the Interior <https://www.nps.gov/sajh/learn/historyculture/the-redoubt.htm>.

P. 158 gathering of lady bug beetles: Vernon. 2010. p. 54.

P. 158 Indigenous people cultivated camas: Suttles, Wayne Prescott. 1951. *Economic Life of the Coast Salish of Haro and Rosario Straits*. Thesis submitted to the University of Washington. This thesis is one of the best early treatments of this activity.

P. 158 Sheep dip trough: Personal communication, Boyd Pratt. October November 7, 2018.

P. 159 The county road: Vouri, Mike & Julia. 2010. *Images of America, San Juan Island.* Arcadia Publishing: Charleston, South Carolina. p. 104.

P. 160 "… on a nippy October morning …": Dawson. 1909. Vol 1. No. 22.

P. 160 reindeer lichen: *Cladina rangiferina.* Kozloff, Eugene N. 1976. *Plants and Animals of the Pacific Northwest.* University of Washington Press. p. 155. Often called reindeer moss because it was one of the lichens eaten by reindeer in Arctic regions.

Bluebirds in the Rain

P. 167 western bluebird: *Sialia mexicana* is a songbird of the Family Turdidae (thrush). It was first described in 1832 by Swainson. In the west, the blues are permanent residents in the southwest including California, Arizona and south to Vera Cruz Mexico. Many Washington State blues migrate south in the winter as far as central Mexico depending on available food.

P. 171 they purchased: Environmental Site Assessment, Phase I, Gann Ranch 290 Valley Grand Farms Road March 9, 2012 for SJPT.

P. 171 "not even a Russian duke …": *Seattle Times*, August 13, 1990 / E2 *Ganns donate land for preservation" by Ann Do.*

P. 171 It's a wonderful thing: San Juan Preservation Trust video. Land Conservation Stories: "Dodie Gann: Red Mill Farm", San Juan Island. Photography, Audio and Multimedia produced by Jane K. Fox. March 13, 2012.

P. 172 decline of the oaks: Doug McCutchen personal communication.

P. 173 flocks of these birds: Lewis and Sharpe. 1987. p. 164.

P. 173 last reported breeding pair: Lewis and Sharpe. 1987. Note 93. p. 205.

P. 173 several organizations: Ecostudies International, the American Bird Conservancy, San Juan Audubon Society, and Joint Base Lewis-McChord (JBLM).

P. 173 Foley-Lewis: At the time of this writing Foley-Lewis was Stewardship Manager for The Trust. She later acquired the title of Conservation Projects manager.

P. 174 Salish Seeds Nursery: San Juan County Conservation Land Bank project conceived and developed and managed by botanist Eliza Habegger.

P. 176 the hue of the earth on its breast ...": Burroughs, John. 1904. *The Writings of John Burroughs*, Chapter VII (p. 205), Houghton Mifflin & Co. 1904 < https://libquotes.com/john-burroughs/quote/lby3d9e >.

P. 177 bluebirds recently hatched: incubation 12-18 days; fledge 18-25 days; total days egg to flight 30- 43.

P. 178 They linger like the leaves: Neltje Blanchan, *Bird Neighbors*, 1904. Garden City Publishing: Garden City, New York. p. 100.

P. 181 carried the sky on its back: Henry David Thoreau excerpt from:https://mdc.mo.gov/blogs/discover-nature-notes/bird-sky-its-back-<0#:~:text=Poet%20Henry%20David%20Thoreau%20wrote%20that%20the%20bluebird,bluebirds%20once%20made%20their%20homes%20in%20tree%20cavities.>. Missouri Department of Conservation. "The Bird with the Sky on its Back." From Discover Nature Notes, March 17, 2019.

P. 181 Post Script: https://sjpt.org/bluebirds-nest-au-naturel/ July 22, 2022.

Searching for Spring

P. 183 Satin flower (*Olsynium douglasaii* aka *Sisyrinchium douglasaii)* is a member of the Iris Family. It was first described: (A. Dietr.) E.P. Bicknell. While relatively common in some regions of the Puget lowlands, it is still specialized in the islands.

P. 188 Kulshan: present-day Mt. Baker. <https://www.tribalpedia.com/us-tribes/a-l/lummi-nation/.> "Bride of the Pacific".

Bidding Adieu

P. 194 It was heartening to learn: Personal communication with Joe Buchanan of Washington State Department of Fish and Wildlife. May 28, 2023.

P. 196 "Surely a Short-eared Owl …": Dawson, William, 1909. Vol 2. No.183, page 464. https://archive.org/details/birdsofwashingto02daws/page/464/mode/2up p. 464, accessed April 2023.

P. 196 northern harrier: *Circus hudsonius* is a raptor in the Family Accipitridae. It was first described by Linnaeus in 1766. This medium-sized, ground-nesting hawk, formerly known as marsh hawk, is found in open habitats and wetlands. In Washington State, they breed primarily in the east with some birds nesting in the Puget Trough and south coast. Migrants may winter in the San Juans. Harriers feed primarily on small mammals and small birds.

P. 198 red-tailed hawk: *Buteo jamaicensis* is a raptor in the Family Accipitridae. It was first described by Gmelin in 1788. Red-tails are common world wide and occupy a wide range of open terrain and woodland edges. They are opportunistic predators on San Juan Island feeding mainly on small mammals such as mice, voles and rabbits. This is a medium-sized hawks of three and one- half pounds with a wing span that may reach 4.5 feet. Females are 25% larger than males.

P. 199 "the wonder of flight …": Dawson, William. 1909, Vol 2. No. 205, page 506. https://archive.org/details/birdsofwashingto02daws/page/504/mode/2up. Accessed April 2023.

Note: Some material in this book was derived from the author's *San Juan Nature Notebook* columns, published by the *San Juan Islander* from 1998 to 2016. The events depicted here took place over a span of several years and were arranged seasonally to create a sense of continuity for the reader.

References

Atkinson, Scott and Fred Sharpe. 1985. *Wild Plants of the San Juan Islands.* The Mountaineers: Seattle.

Avery, Christy. 2016. *San Juan Island National Historical Park - An Environmental History.* U.S. National Park Service, Pacific West Regional Office. Seattle, Washington.

Baicich, Paul J. and Colin J. O. Harrison. 1997. *A Guide to the Nests, Eggs, and Nestlings of North American Birds* (Second Edition). Academic Press: San Diego.

Blanchan, Neltje.1897. *Bird Neighbors.* Garden City Publishing Inc.: Garden City, New Jersey.

Clark, Lewis J. 1976. *Wild Flowers of the Pacific Northwest.* Gray's Publishing Limited: Sidney, British Columbia Canada.

Cooper, Susan Fenimore. 1850. *Rural Hours,* Edited by Rochelle Johnson and Daniel Patterson. University of Georgia Press: Athens. USA. 1998. < https://doi.org/10.2173/bna.615> .

Dawson, W.L. & J.H Bowles. 1909. *Birds of Washington, A Complete Scientific and Popular Account of the 372 Species of Birds Found in the State.* Occidental Pub Co. Seattle.

Domico, Terry. 1998. *Lime Kiln Quarries Property, San Juan Island, San Juan County, Washington. Puget Sound BioSurvey*: Seattle, WA.

Geographical Memoir of the Islands Between the Continent and Vancouver Island in the Vicinity of the Forty-Ninth Parallel of North Latitude, October 1868; 40th Congress, 2nd Session, Ex Doc No. 29. Archibald Campbell, with appendices (not published) by Dr.

C.B.R Kennerly, George Gibbs, Henry Custer, and William J. Warren. Handwritten copies of the appendices on file with the San Juan Island National Historical Park. Friday Harbor, Washington at the time of research.

Goguen, B. and D. R. Curson. 2002. Cassin's Vireo (*Vireo cassinii*), version 2.0. In *The Birds of North America* (A. F. Poole and F. B. Gill, Editors). Cornell Lab of Ornithology, Ithaca, NY. <http://bna.birds.cornell.edu/bna/species/615doi:10.2173/bna.615; >.

Gunther, Edna. 1945. *Ethnobotany of Western Washington*. University of Washington Press: Seattle.

Guppy, C.S. and J.H. Shepard. 2001. *Butterflies of British Columbia: Including Western Alberts, Southern Yukon, the Alaska Panhandle, Washington, Northern Oregon, Northern Idaho, and Northwestern Montana.* UBC Press: Vancouver, B.C.

Hanson, Thor. 2011. *Feathers*. Basic Books: New York.

Haskin, Leslie L. 1967. *Wild Flowers of the Pacific Coast*, Binford & Mort: Portland, Oregon.

Hinchcliff, John. 1996. *An Atlas of Washington Butterflies.* The Evergreen Aurelians. The Oregon State University Bookstore, Inc.: Corvallis.

James David G. and David Nunnallee. 2011. *Life Histories of Cascadia Butterflies.* Oregon State University Press: Corvallis.

Kozloff, Eugene N. 1976. *Plants and Animals of the Pacific Northwest*. University of Washington Press: Seattle.

Lewis, Mark and Fred A. Sharpe. 1987. *Birding in the San Juan Islands*. The Mountaineers: Seattle.

McLellan, Roy Davidson. 1927. *The Geology of the San Juan Islands*. University of Washington Press: Seattle.

Newcombe, C.F. 1923. *Menzies' Journal of Vancouver's Voyage.* Archives of British Columbia. Victoria, B.C.

Paulson, Dennis. 1993. *Shorebirds of the Pacific Northwest*. University of Washington Press: Seattle.

_____. 1999. *Dragonflies of Washington*. Seattle Audubon Society: Seattle.

_____. 2009. *Dragonflies and Damselflies of the West*, Princeton University Press: Princeton.

Pearson, T. Gilbert (Editor in Chief). 1917. *Birds of America*. The University Society, Inc.: New York.

Pratt, Boyd C. 2016. *LIME, Quarrying and Limemaking in the San Juan Islands*. Mulno Cove Publishing: Friday Harbor.

_____. 2014. *Limestone Quarrying and Limemaking in the San Juan Islands*. <HistoryLink.org 10935>.

_____. 2021. *ISLAND FISHING History and Seascape of Marine Harvesting in the San Juan Islands amid the Salish Sea*. Mulno Cove Publishing: Friday Harbor.

Pojar, Jim and Andy MacKinnon. 2004. *Plants of the Pacific Northwest Coast, Washington, Oregon, British Columbia & Alaska*. Lone Pine Publishing: Vancouver, British Columbia.

Pyle, Robert Michael. 1992. *Handbook for Butterfly Watchers*. Houghton Mifflin Company: Boston.

_____. 2002. *The Butterflies of Cascadia, A Field Guide to all Species of Washington, Oregon and Surrounding Territories*. Seattle Audubon Society: Seattle.

Pyle, Robert Michael and C. LaBar. 2018. *Butterflies of the Pacific Northwest*. Timber Press: Portland, Oregon.

Schroeder, Tom, 2007. *Rediscovering A Coastal Prairie Near Friday Harbor*. <http://www.rockisland.com/~tom?LostPrairie.html>.

Sibley, David. 2000. *The Sibley Guide to Birds*. Alfred A. Knopf: New York.

Sierra College, Journal of the Natural History Museum, Sierra College website; Journal of the Sierra College Natural History Museum. Frances Theodora Parsons: <https://www.sierracollege.edu/ejournals/jscnhm/v6n1/parsons.html>. Accessed, November 16, 2021.

Starr-Dana, Mrs. William. 1989, *How to Know the Wild Flowers*. Houghton Mifflin Company. Boston. p. 65. Originally published in 1893 by Charles Scribner's Sons.

Suttles, Wayne Prescott. 1951. *Economic Life of the Coast Salish of Haro and Rosario Straits*. Thesis submitted to the University of Washington.

Vernon, Susan. 1997. *Birds of American Camp – Checklist /* San Juan Island National Historical Park. ArchipelagoPress: Friday Harbor, WA.

_____. 1998. *Wildlife of the San Juan Islands – Checklist*. Archipelago Press: Friday Harbor, WA.

_____. 2001. *Notes on the Occurrence of Butterflies at Cattle Point NRCA, San Juan Island, Washington*. unpublished report to the Washington Department of Fish and Wildlife/Department of Wildlife.

_____. 2005. *Birds of Cattle Point NRCA – Checklist*. Washington. Department of Natural Resources, (DNR): Olympia, Washington.

_____. 2007. *Butterflies of San Juan Island – Checklist*. Archipelago Press: Friday Harbor, WA.

_____. 2010. *Rainshadow World – A Naturalist's Year in the San Juan Islands*. Archipelago Press: Friday Harbor, WA.

Vouri, Mike, 2008. *The Pig War*. Arcadia Publishing: Charleston, South Carolina.

_____. 2018. *Salmon Bank*. <www.historylink.org/FILE20510>.

Wray, Jacilee. 2003. *The Salmon Bank – An Ethnohistoric Compilation*. Anthropologist North Coast and Cascades Network for San Juan National Historical Park.

Acknowledgments

I am grateful to the following individuals and organizations for their information, expertise, council, support and congeniality throughout the field work and writing of this book.

Katherine Gunther for her invaluable guidance and support during my early years on San Juan Island doing field work and interpretation with the Washington Department of Natural Resources at Cypress Island and the Cattle Point NRCA.

Julie Combs, John Fleckenstein, Amy Lambert, Kathleen Foley Lewis, Ruth Milner, Ann Potter, Karen Reagan and Lee Taylor for collaboration and information during my field work with the island marble butterfly, sand-verbena moth and western bluebirds. And to Trent Lieber and Claire Crawbuck for taking such good care of American Camp wildlife for the National Park Service in recent times under the guidance of Elexis Fredy and Sara Dolan.

Joe Buchanan, Eliza Habegger, Thor Hanson, Kurt License, Doug McCutchen, Dennis Paulson, Boyd Pratt and Mike Vouri for consults on species identification, island history and natural history.

To Shona Aitken and the kind folks at Wolf Hollow Wildlife Rehabilitation Center for their unwavering care of island wildlife especially Songbird #10-452. And to the San Juan Island Library for providing, over many years, invaluable support that significantly enhanced this work.

I was inspired in immeasurable ways by Eugene N. Kozloff and Louisa Nishitani who taught me both in the field and in personal encounters about botany and the undeniable joys of leading a life filled with generosity of spirit.

I am especially grateful to Jean Shreve, my birding pal, for her superb counsel, keen perspective on island wildlife, and invaluable comments on the manuscript from its earliest stages. To Emily Geyman for her impeccable eye and thoughtful ideas. To Eileen Drath and Larry Wight for their feedback and support as readers. And to Nancy Spaulding for her meticulous read and, most importantly, for her wisdom and friendship (with Lewis) over the decades of our island adventures. Rebecca Cook's contributions to the production of this book were numerous. Her artistic skills and keen technicality created a beautiful and inviting design.

To Rosie the Barn Cat for her excellent company on many birding walks near home.

Foremost, my deepest gratitude to Miss May and Vera Darlene's mom—my dear friend—whose encouragement to move to the San Juan Islands many years ago began the most remarkable and happy phase of my life.

Any errors in this storytelling are mine alone.

Permissions

Grateful acknowledgment is made to the following for permission to print previously published material or excerpts from unpublished reports under copyright.

Robert Michael Pyle from *The Butterflies of Cascadia, A Field Guide to all Species of Washington, Oregon and Surrounding Territories* by Robert Michael Pyle. Page 182. published by the Seattle Audubon Society.

Tom Schroeder from Schroeder, Tom, 2007. *Rediscovering A Coastal Prairie Near Friday Harbor*, <http://www.rockisland.com/~tom?LostPrairie.html>.

Credits

All photographs are by Susan Vernon except for the American Avocet, a public domain image from the U.S. Geological Survey. https://www.usgs.gov/media/images/american-avocet-2. Sandra Uecker, USFWS.

Index

About the Author

Susan Vernon is the author of *Rainshadow World—A Naturalist's Year in the San Juan Islands.* She is a Pacific Northwest native having lived in the islands for over thirty years as the executive director of a small natural history museum, co-founder of the San Juan Nature Institute, land steward, interpretive specialist, and consulting naturalist for several government agencies and the San Juan Preservation Trust. Susan conducted surveys for the endangered island marble butterfly for over fifteen years and developed the first captive rearing protocol for the subspecies. Her column *San Juan Nature Notebook* appeared for many years in the local press.

www.ingramcontent.com/pod-product-compliance
Lightning Source LLC
Chambersburg PA
CBHW072117020426
42334CB00018B/1626